Maid in America

BOOK TWO OF THE *MAN MAID* SERIES

AURORA ALBA

BOOK TWO OF THE *MAN MAID* SERIES

For Erica.

Thank you for working endlessly to make all of my work shine.

And to all of you beautifully imperfect people out there, you have my love and respect.

Content Warning:

This novel contains profanity, discussions of mood disorders, depression, and suicide. It also contains some drug and alcohol use, & sexually graphic descriptions.

I

"Barrett," slurred a shaggy-haired man in his twenties, swaying as he waited. "Get your ass over here."

Barrett removed his tan jacket, exposing the tight, muscle-hugging T-shirt beneath, and tossed it onto a wooden bar stool nearby before embracing the man. "What's up, Anthony? Where's your better half?"

Anthony groaned, chugged another shot, and slammed the empty glass onto the bar, startling a nearby cluster of women.

Barrett flashed an apologetic glance to a busty blonde across the table sporting a faded black tank with the iconic logo of AC/DC splashed across the front. She winked back at him as Anthony stretched.

"Linda got pissed off. Took the kids and went to her Mom's in El Paso on Tuesday."

Barrett tore his eyes away from the thirsty blonde long enough to give Anthony a pointed glare. "Oh yeah? What'd you do *this* time?"

"Why are you assuming I was the one to fuck up? You're supposed to be *my* friend."

Barrett slung his arm around Anthony's sagging shoulders. "I am your friend, bud, but *good* friends sometimes gotta smack the shit outta you when you're bein' stupid. What'd you do?"

"She's actin' like I screwed someone."

"Well? Did you?"

"No!"

Barrett sighed and pulled his buddy in tighter. "Look, you and Linda are good together. You've been together for a goddamned decade now. Don't throw it away over you being an ass."

"Why do you assume I was an ass?"

"Because I know you, Anthony. You are an ass. A lovable ass, but an ass all the same. You want my advice?"

"No."

"My advice? Sober the hell up, pack a bag and hit the road tomorrow. Grovel, if you have to. And don't forget to bring a big ass bouquet of flowers. She likes carnations if memory serves."

Anthony shrugged off Barrett's comment. "Dude, not you, too."

"What?" Barrett eyed his friend and subtly scanned the room.

"You, Char, my Dad... everyone's acting like I'm supposed to chase her down and make some grand gesture."

4

"So *do it*, numb nuts!" Barrett shoved him hard but playful.

Anthony regained his stance and frowned. "Barrett, tonight I'm putting that shit out of my head, and I'm cuttin' loose. No fuckin' Linda telling me what to do and where I should be. No kids whining and bitching about one wanting the other one's fuckin' toy." He sighed. "Is this what your life's like all the time? Carefree? On the hunt for undiscovered poon?"

"Yup." Barrett flashed a brilliant smile at a curvaceous brunette passing by. "Pretty much."

Barrett inhaled the scent of cheap whiskey, old cedar, discarded peanut shells, and dried hay around him. *The Hole* was, in his opinion, the only truly authentic western honky tonk joint within at least sixty miles of Jackson. A massive dance floor sat at its center, clustered with smiling cowgirls in wide-brimmed hats and grim-faced men in tight Wranglers and pricey Ariats. Atop the worn wood, a mob of people spun and twirled, line dancing to the upbeat rhythm of the country music blaring through the amps. The dark plank walls bore neon logos of every alcohol brand a Wyomingite could ever desire.

While Jackson Hole was speckled with clubs, a surprising amount for such a small town, *The Hole* was located in the most tourist-laden area. A rushing current of fresh new faces kept the bar a consistently interesting place to cut loose. It provided a constantly revolving pool of new women for Barrett to charm.

He scanned the faces, on the prowl for someone fresh with whom he could temporarily sate his voracious sexual appetite.

Anthony playfully punched him in the bicep. "See anything you like?"

"Ohhhhh yeah."

"Which one?"

"*All of 'em*." Barrett laughed.

Anthony snickered. "Shit, if I had washboard abs like you, my STDs would have STDs."

Barrett barked out a laugh.

Anthony's eyebrows furrowed. "Hey. Where's Will?"

Barrett rolled his eyes. "He and Ava are doing some cake tasting tonight for the wedding. We haven't hung out in weeks."

"Shit, soon, he'll be another brother lost to marital hell, anchored by a ball and chain, drowning at the bottom of the suburban ocean with the rest of us dumb assholes, the poor *schmuck*."

"Well, aren't you a little ball of optimism tonight?" Barrett joked.

Anthony slapped Barrett on the back so hard it stung. "I'm gonna do a round and mingle. Catch you later, man."

As Anthony darted off into the packed swarm of people near the bar, Barrett cupped a hand and yelled over Luke Bryan's voice, asking country girls to shake it for him, "Don't be an idiot! Pull your head out of your ass and go get Linda back!"

Anthony scoffed and disappeared into the crowd.

Barrett leaned back on the bar and nodded at the blonde in the AC/DC shirt. She and the two women beside her gawked, laughed, and waved. He flashed another knee-weakening smile at all three, watching the women melt before his mocha-colored eyes.

Like fishing with dynamite.

He turned back to the bar, flagging down Daisy, the pissy bartender. She grimaced, letting out a dramatic grunt as she reluctantly approached, wiping sloppy liquid dribbles off the bar top the whole way. Her stormy eyes narrowed at the sight of him.

"*Barrett.*" There was ice in her tone, like that of an agitated phone sex operator, equal parts sensual and frigid.

"Awww, come on, Daisy. You aren't *still* mad at me, are you?"

Her furious glare gave him the only answer he needed. He watched her shapely ass as she twisted to retrieve a bottle behind her, the silky skin of her tapered waist taunting him through the gap between her crop top and painted-on frayed jeans. She whipped back up, catching his eyes settling on her cleavage.

She pointed the neck of a bottle of Maker's Mark at him like an accusatory finger. "Fuck off, Barrett."

"Is that any way to talk to a regular?" He smiled, but she was impervious to his charm. Jaded, like many others in his sexual wake. He was great at getting women, even better at ghosting them.

He held up two calloused palms defensively. "I'll just take a double of Wyomin' Whiskey, neat, and get outta your hair." He swallowed. "Which looks really nice today, by the way."

Daisy flipped her caramel ponytail over her shoulder and huffed. Teeth gritted, she snatched a nearby glass and a bottle of his favorite local whiskey. After pouring two fingers of booze, she sloshed the glass across the scuffed wooden bar top at him.

"For *you*, that'll be twenty-five bucks."

Barrett pressed his lips together and nodded. "On second thought, I shouldn't drink tonight. I'm driving."

Daisy shook her head and snatched the drink back from the counter. "Suit yourself."

She swallowed the contents of the glass herself and then set the cup in the sink behind the bar, never breaking eye contact with him. He opened his mouth to reply, but he knew no words could remove the foot he'd already planted there when he snuck out of her house the week prior.

It was time to institute a new rule: *Never fuck the bartender.* He added it to the lengthy list of mistakes he'd made over the years.

Luckily, in a tourist town, there were always fresh faces, women who had no clue about the reputation that preceded him, one that dried up panties and sent sensible women racing for the door.

As he turned back to the dance floor, an arm snaked around his own, squeezing like a python.

"Hey, babe, this is Mark. He just bought me a drink. Ain't that the sweetest thing?" the female voice cooed.

Barrett turned to see an unfamiliar face gazing up at him from their several-inch height difference. She was a stunning creature, the kind of woman that the bards of old wrote songs about. Her arresting amber eyes blinked up at him, hypnotic beneath the shimmering beams of the overhead par-cans. Her delicious-looking lips were highly glossed and twisted into a nervous smile. Her shoulder-length hair was dyed in blended bands of rainbow colors coiled around her delicate face in breezy curls.

For once, Barrett felt too dumbstruck to be suave.

Rising on her toes to close the height gap between them, she leaned closer to his ear. He caught a hint of her jasmine perfume as she whispered, *"Please go with it. This dipshit won't leave me the hell alone."*

Barrett nodded and glanced at the intoxicated man hovering in her personal space. His posture straightened, and he cast a threatening glance despite the casual smile spread across his mouth. "Nice to meet you."

"Mark is in tractor sales. Isn't that fun, honey?" she asked. She motioned to the leathery fifty-something in a white Stetson, plaid shirt pulled taut over his protruding gut.

Barrett stared down into her stunning eyes. "Baby, don't settle for table scraps when you got prime rib right here."

"Pfft. Fuckin' *cocktease*." The bedraggled man grumbled, waving her away. Then, he looked at Barrett like he wanted a fight. "Who the fuck you callin' 'table scraps,' asshole?!"

Barrett flexed, standing rigid and ready to pulverize the man. He stepped toward him, hovering nearly a foot taller. *"Mark*, was it?

Mark, if you so much as *look* in my woman's direction again, I will hit you so fucking hard, you'll shit your own molars."

Barrett's heart raced excitedly at the notion, at the familiar, invigorating feeling of his knuckles colliding violently with a man's skin and bone, sweet pain radiating back through his extremities. His hands twitched, fingers aching to ball into fists.

The man gritted his teeth and swatted the air between them. "Ain't about to catch a case over some dumb cunt like her. You can keep her."

Normally, Barrett would have given chase, dragged the old man out to the parking lot, and made him eat a curb. But tonight, he wanted to stay with the alluring temptress, the one trying to hide her gorgeous smile with a cupped hand.

As the man disappeared into the crowd, she broke into giggles.

Barrett looked down and smiled. "You like the idea of an old man getting his ass put in the ICU over you?"

She looked Barrett up and down, taking all of him in for the first time. He was all too aware of that look. The lust, the stunned amazement, his muscular frame stoking flames of red hot heat that always seemed to flush women's cheeks.

But she seemed... *different*. She seemed like someone whose smile could not be easily forgotten when the morning sun arose, and the flattering haze of beer goggles had lifted. Hers was a face he wanted to memorize, a rare gem among a shoreline of pebbles, eyes sparkling with a brilliance that made time stand still.

"You got a name?" he finally managed, staring, lost in the allure of her velvet lips. He could picture himself parting them with his tongue and suddenly wondered what flavor of gloss she wore.

She smiled, one infused with a tempting mixture of mischief and chaos. "Aphrodite."

He rubbed his fingers through the neatly shorn stubble on his chin. "Either your parents have an odd sense of humor, or you're screwing with me."

She shrugged and smiled playfully. "Maybe it's my name. Maybe it isn't. Either way, it keeps things exciting."

"Well, *Aphrodite*," he said mockingly, "if that ugly prick bothers you again, come find me."

She laughed. The sound was pure and sweet, something he wanted to make her again.

And again...

"Barrett, right?" She stuffed her hands into her back pockets. "I overheard someone call you that a few minutes ago."

Her wicked grin made heat bloom through his groin, hardening his cock as he wrapped one of her rainbow-colored curls around a rough finger. "Oh, it's *Adonis,* actually."

Her breath caught as Barrett's knuckle grazed her cheek. She swallowed hard, losing some of her steely resolve. He waited for her to shy away from his hand, but she leaned against it instead. "Mighty high opinion of yourself."

He leaned down and brushed his lips against her ear. "Can't you see, Aphrodite? You and me… it's *fate.*"

She chuckled and crossed her arms over her breasts.

"Right. Well, *Adonis*, thank you for helping me ditch that guy." She patted her palm on his chest, shocked by the marble-hard muscle beneath his shirt. She resisted the desire to let her eyes widen in shock, to ruin the cool facade she'd established. "Enjoy the rest of your night."

"Alright." A pang of disappointment plummeted down into the pit of Barrett's stomach.

"Stay away from wild boars," she joked.

He scrunched his brows. "Excuse me?"

She replied with a laugh. "You must not know your Greek mythology very well."

"You got me there." He licked his bottom lip and forced a laugh as she waltzed backward toward rows of line dancers. "See you around, Aphrodite."

"Maybe." She shrugged and spun, chunky boot heels clacking out onto the weathered dance floor, ass swaying like a metronome to the lively beat.

Barrett sighed and returned to the bar, trying to shake Aphrodite from his mind as the twang of steel guitars and crooning voices dribbled from the amps.

Soon, a busty woman wearing a fringe skirt breezed past. She winked, drinking in the image of Barrett's body like water in Saharan sand. His smile was quick to fade. He knew her. They'd been to bed together at some point in the last year. It was all becoming a blur of faces.

Jackson Hole wasn't the smallest town in Wyoming, but in the decade Barrett had lived there, many faces had stayed the same. In fact, too many for his liking.

His eyes scanned the room. Watching. Assessing. He took a visual inventory of every woman in the establishment, imagining each one as a one-of-a-kind sensual snowflake he could confidently melt with his tongue.

As his gaze wandered, his sight returned to the rainbow-haired beauty, now chatting with another man in a *No Fear* T-shirt and a mesh trucker's hat. She pushed the man away playfully, throwing her head back in a hearty laugh.

Something inside squeezed its frustrated claws around Barrett's gut, wrenching hard at the display. *He* wanted to be the one to coax that beautiful sound from her. He watched for a moment as her fingers trailed along the man's chest, prancing like the graceful feet of a ballet dancer down the front. Every tap of contact pulled at Barrett like a cord, tugging him toward her before he could stop himself. As he wound his way through the crowd in her direction, he was caught by the arm.

"Hey!" squeaked a drunken woman as she hopped off her stool, nearly falling over on dismount. Barrett caught her just in time before she tumbled to the shell-covered floor.

He glanced down at her face, trying desperately to remember her name.

Shauna?

Barbara?

Something with an 'ah' at the end…

"Barrett?! What are you doing here? I thought you ssssaid you were done with the bar scene," she slurred, eyes narrow slits.

"Old habits die hard, I'm afraid." He gave her a moment to steady herself on her rhinestoned heels.

"These guys are amazing. This is my *song*!" she screamed, pointing at the high ceiling.

"I don't think I've heard this band before. Who are they?" Barrett asked, reeling back when the woman - *Carla maybe?* - spun around with a look of utter shock. Her beautiful, tan face contorted into a mouth-open gape of someone who had just watched him slap a kitten.

"It's *Lonesome Creek*! How do you not know this band?!"

"I guess I don't pay much attention to music these days."

Diana? Her name *had* to be Diana.

Probably.

The woman reached up, snatched his shirt collar in her petite hand, and tugged his face toward hers. The overpowering odor of cranberry and gin wafted at him in a boozy gust.

"You should come over. I'll play some of their music for you." Her intoxicated attempt at seduction was barely audible above the tune.

Barrett's hand gently plucked her grip from his shirt. "Maybe another time. You're drunk."

"So?!"

"Darlin', the only thing you need to be suckin' on in your bed tonight is a big bottle of water."

She honked out a laugh, and her eyes squinted further. "Party pooper! Rain-check?"

She jabbed him in the chest with a pointed finger more forcefully than he'd anticipated.

He grabbed her by the offending hand and placed a soft kiss on the back of it. "We'll see."

She waved him away, shrieking like a dying eagle as the DJ played the next song, another recent chart topper.

Barrett shuffled through the crowd and eventually walked up behind Aphrodite. He darted through a too-small pocket of space behind her, intentionally bumping her forward with a jolt. She spilled her drink on the front of the man's T-shirt, and he jumped back dramatically, arms out like Jesus, face instantly twisted into a look of fury.

"What the *fuck?*" he snarled, swiping at his soaked clothes.

"Ah shit," Barrett said, slapping a hand on the man's back. "Hell, man, I'm sorry. My bad. I'm like a bull in a China shop. Here." Barrett plucked a ten-dollar bill from the calfskin wallet in his back pocket. He slid a hand subtly around Aphrodite's waist and waved the money at the drenched stranger. "*That* drink is on you. Next one's on *me*."

With a scowl, the man snatched the ten-spot, glowered at Barrett, and then stomped off toward the bathroom, mouth moving as he muttered every conceivable curse word.

Aphrodite turned to Barrett, feeling his firm hand slip around her back to the other side of her waist, buzzing at his touch.

"That wasn't an accident, was it?" Her eyes flicked to his, a smirk showcased across her cheeks.

He shook his head, refusing to blink as he studied her stunning face.

"Hmmm. This is fun," she said. "Maybe I should find another guy who looks like trouble so I can watch you in action again."

"Oh, you *like* that kind of thing, do you?"

She could feel the low bass of Barrett's velvet voice rumble from his body. She nodded, momentarily unable to form words.

"Well, play your cards right, and by the end of the night, I'll end up kicking some poor sap's ass all the way outta town for makin' extended eye contact with a Goddess like you."

"*You're* making extended eye contact," she finally said, her body inching toward his, the fabric of their jeans rubbing.

"Yes. But I'm Adonis, remember? These other men..." He looked around, "Mere *mortals*."

She stepped back, and he moved forward, once again closing the gap between them.

"Wanna dance?" he asked, his eyes flicking down to her lips and back up to her face.

"Feels like we already are."

Barrett chuckled, never taking his eyes off her.

"See if you can keep up," she yelled, leading him onto the dance floor. Her touch sent a shock pulsing through him.

He spun her, tethering Aphrodite with a light grasp before recoiling her shoulders back into his strong arms. She pressed herself against his body as if they had been molded to fit one another perfectly.

"*God damn, Aphrodite,*" Barrett mumbled, embracing her intimately, hoping his sudden proclamation of pleasant surprise would be drowned out by the pulsing drumbeats.

"You're not so bad *yourself,*" she muttered between deep breaths.

"How come I've never seen you out here before?" He asked, feeling thrown off-balance. The heady mixture of her perfume and the way her eyes bored into him made him feel three whiskeys deep.

"I haven't been around for a while." She grinned. "What? Why are you looking at me like that? I can't tell if you're scared or turned on."

He laughed. "Both."

"Don't be afraid. I don't bite unless you *want* me to," she teased, spinning out again and returning to his chest.

"Oh, I *want* you to, Aphrodite. I *dare* you to."

Her carefree laugh was melodic and uplifting. The sound of it made his whole day melt away.

Barrett craned his neck and leaned in close, breath fluttering against the shell of her ear, sending a shiver down her spine. "Wanna get out of here?"

She tried to hide her smile, jutting her jaw as she looked around. "What kinda girl do you think I am?"

"You're a little firecracker," he growled into her ear. "Dangerous as hell and *truly* a beautiful sight to behold."

"I'll bet you say that to all the girls."

He shook his head close to her face, his nose nearly brushing hers. "Just you."

"Surrrrrre." She giggled, tapping her forehead against the hollow of his throat.

"You know, Aphrodite," he said, holding her closer, "*I'm* not one to beg, but if you give me a chance to show you what I can do off the dance floor," he flashed a cocky grin, "*you* just might."

That kind of confidence was her secret weakness. Her spine went rigid, knees unsteady. She felt any possible witty retort evaporate the instant he uttered it.

Barrett could swear she was blushing, could feel her weakened gait as they danced. The thought of having that kind of effect on her made him even more aware of his growing erection, one starting to rage against the stiff barrier of his tight jeans. One he was sure she could feel as he dipped her backward, feeling her thigh sink between his.

"Suppose I said 'yes,'" she said. "Where would we go?"

"My place." His hands trailed down her arms.

"Well, then, what are we waiting for?" She bit her bottom lip.

Without another word, he slid a hand behind the small of her back and whispered, "*Get your things.*"

In the parking lot, men cackled in the distance, deep in some sort of intoxicated conversation with one another. Barrett pointed to his black Jeep, one with mud-encrusted tires in desperate need of a good scrub-down. "You wanna ride with me or follow?"

"I'll follow. I don't do sleepovers," she said, unlocking a sedan a few vehicles away with the key fob in her hand.

"Honey," he grinned, pausing to devour every inch of her with his eyes, "With a body like that in my apartment, I wouldn't *fathom* sleeping."

2

The door to Barrett's studio apartment swung open to reveal a modest loft with red support beams and exposed brick walls. It smelled faintly of sweat and cologne. The open expanse was decorated with mismatched leather furniture and littered with laundry, cowboy boots, and half-full water bottles. The counter was full of strewn papers, surfaces speckled with bits of food and water rings from perspired glasses.

The moment the apartment door clicked shut, Barrett hung his keys on one of the prongs on his mounted jackalope head by the entrance. The taxidermied rabbit's head adorned with glued-on antlers stared back at them, a gift his grandmother had given him as a housewarming present years prior.

Barrett grabbed Aphrodite's hands and pinned them over her head against the brick wall just inside the front door. He pressed his mouth to hers for a deep kiss and then trailed smaller, softer ones down her chin and neck, skimming across her collarbone with his eager mouth.

She panted, arms slackening in his grasp as he softly nipped at her jaw and bottom lip. She moaned, loud and fierce.

Barrett thought about his neighbors down the hall and how they were desensitized to the female voices coming from his apartment by now. Their averted, bashful gazes in the laundry room were something he took pride in.

"Mmmm. That fucking moan, girl. Do that again. I liked it," he groaned, voice gravelly. His eyes grew dark, hooded by a thick veil of desire.

"*Make me.*"

The taunt sent a bolt of heat to his groin.

"I do like a feisty woman," he said gruffly, the corner of his lip twitching up onto a half-smile. He released her hands, backed away, and headed toward the kitchen.

"Wow." She made her way to the center of the apartment, looking around at several hung paintings of the nude female form and the occasional framed photo. "I like your place. I love these old buildings; they have such a *vibe*."

"A *vibe*?" he asked from the open kitchen. "What kind of a *vibe* are you getting from this place?"

"It has a sort of stylish industrial charm to it. I bet it gets gorgeous light during the day."

He watched, unable to take his eyes off the way her colorful hair danced against her shoulders.

She circled his weight bench in the corner, still racked with fifty-pound weights, clacking her nails against the metal bar as she passed it.

She stopped in the middle of a bank of windows, soaking in the town's main thoroughfare below. A few run-down cars peppered the roadway, and drunken patrons meandered down the sidewalks. The lights of Jackson twinkled like fireflies in the dark night sky.

"It's a great view," Barrett said, making his way to her, pressing himself softly against her back and wrapping a strong arm around to offer her a beveled glass of booze.

"No, thanks." She shook her head, only peeling her eyes from the stunning view long enough to decline.

Barrett shrugged and poured her drink into his. He set the empty on the brick sill and leaned against the window, staring at her as he sipped.

She strode toward him, nudging between his bent knees with her leg to get closer.

Something about being near her sent a prick of sweat to the back of Barrett's neck, the embers between them stoking hotter every time they touched. He slid a flattened hand to her stomach, and she tensed.

"What's your real name, Aphrodite?" he asked, stroking the tender skin there.

"I've already told you the only name you're going to get."

"Hmm," Barrett pulled his hand away and brought the bitter amber liquid back to his lips. "So, Aphrodite, what do you do for work?"

"Do you really want to talk about work right now?" She stepped away, waltzing toward his leather couch and sitting in it like royalty on a throne.

"If I can guess what you do for a living, will you tell me?" Barrett stared for a moment, eyes locked on her body, overwhelmed by an insatiable urge to taste her.

She looked away. "Why not? I'll grant you three guesses."

"Thank you, sexy genie."

She fought a smile.

"Guess one: you're the hottest DJ Wyoming has ever seen. DJ Greek Goddess is your moniker."

"*Oooooh*. So close!" She held her fingers a centimeter apart. "Two left."

"Okay. You're not a DJ. No, I was way off. You're a Wyoming Cowboys cheerleader?"

She shook her head.

"No. Dumb guess. You're way too hot for that. Although, there goes my fantasy about finally seducing a cheerleader."

"Why would you want a cheerleader?"

"Because they can do the splits."

"Who said *I* can't?"

Barrett moaned involuntarily and stepped behind the raggedy recliner to hide his growing hard-on.

"Let's see… rainbow hair… you're artistic."

"Hardly."

"You're a photographer, aren't you? You shoot weddings and shit."

"That your final answer?"

"Yep, final answer."

"Wrong. I'm not a photographer…"

"Damn," he muttered.

"But I *am* involved in weddings, actually."

He snapped his fingers and pointed at her. "I knew it."

"I'm in sales. Like insanely overpriced dresses, constrictive suits, painful shoes, and monogrammed hankies for the sobbing helicopter moms."

"The whole nine, huh?" He approached the couch and took another sip of liquor to bolster the courage to sit next to her before finally taking a seat.

"The whole nine." She kicked off her shoes and drew her feet up to the cushion beside her. Her mismatched socks made Barrett chuckle.

He reached out to tap the blue ankle sock on one foot and the pink calf-height one on the other. "Cute."

She looked at them and smiled, allowing her eyes to affix on his. "I guess this is the part where I am supposed to ask about what you do."

"You don't have to." Barrett eyed her feet, desperately wanting to touch them, to rub them, to have them in his lap. "I just started a new job this week, so there isn't much to tell."

"Yeah?" She snuggled into the couch a little more.

"The hours are flexible, which I like. I still want to have fun and live a little, you know? I don't wanna look back and have any regrets. I wanna look like shit by the time I'm in my casket."

"Preach." She picked at a small tear in his sofa absentmindedly with her nail. "Speaking of regrets… you got any tats?"

He laughed aloud. "Now, why would you ask something like that?"

"You strike me as the kinda guy with a hidden thigh sleeve or the quintessential 'Mom' tattoo in a little heart somewhere."

His smile faded at the word 'Mom.' After a moment, it slowly returned. "I actually do have a tattoo. It's small and stupid."

"I *knew* it. I have a sixth sense about these things."

"It's on my butt cheek."

Covering her mouth, Chastity stifled a loud laugh.

"Back in the day, I lost a bet to my buddy, Alan. True to my word, I got it."

"What is it?"

"It's a bumble bee wearing a ghost costume."

She twisted her body to look at him. "*Explain.*"

Barrett stood, unbuttoned his jeans, and pulled them and his underwear down three inches, revealing a two-inch tattoo that looked exactly like he'd described.

"I don't get it."

"*Boo-bee.* It's a boo-bee. Like," he turned and motioned as if he had huge breasts. He couldn't help but smile at Chastity's laughter. He pulled his pants up, re-zipped them, and returned his butt to the couch, inches closer this time.

"What about you? You got any ink?"

"I do."

He waited a moment. "Well…?"

"I have one tattoo, and if you play your cards right, I'll show it to you."

He grinned and made a puckered face like Robert Deniro before taking another sip from his glass. "I'd rather see it anyway."

She held her palm out, silently requesting the glass in his hand.

"I thought you didn't want any." Confused, he handed it over.

"Needed to be sure it wasn't roofied or something. Never can be too careful." She took a big gulp of it.

Barrett scooted closer and reached over, caressing a long curl of rainbow-dyed hair with his outstretched finger. "I like this. It's pretty. Love all the colors."

"Yeah?"

"If I was a bettin' man, I'd guess this is either a post-breakup hairstyle... or you had a strict upbringing."

"Nope," she said quickly, but the lie was apparent on her face. She cleared her throat and averted her eyes. "I just like some vibrancy in my life. I couldn't decide on one color, so I chose them all."

Barrett's bent finger drifted from her hair to her cheek, grazing the flushed flesh of her ear, feeling the heat seeping from her skin.

"I like these, too," he lightly toyed with her earrings. They looked like human rib cages coated in teal epoxy with hot pink hearts dangling inside.

"I like that you're not afraid to stand out. That's sexy."

She smiled, eyes darting away.

"Hey, no, look at me." His voice was soft but stern, echoing out into the quietness of the space.

She forced herself to meet his gaze and smiled. He leaned in slowly, slow enough to allow her to say no, to halt him, or admit she was having second thoughts. But she didn't speak. The only sound between them was the crinkle of leather as he slid his hand up to the back of her neck and pressed his lips firmly to hers.

She kissed him back with a demanding urgency. Her hand wrapped around the back of his neck, and she pulled him closer, savoring the taste of liquor on his warm tongue. Barrett gripped her by the hips and slid her roughly toward him. A small moan escaped her, and he felt the delightful ache grow between his legs.

She grasped the front of his shirt and pulled him against her, digging her nails into his shoulders. He parted her legs with his knees and weaved his fingers into her multi-colored locks.

He moaned against her lips before pulling at the hem of her shirt, hand diving beneath, grazing soft skin with calloused hands.

She shoved her hand between their bodies and massaged his hardened cock through the denim. He gasped and pinched his eyes closed.

"*Mmmmm. Such a naughty girl.*"

"*Mmm-hmmm,*" she purred, stroking harder. She sucked his bottom lip and nibbled, raking her nails down his neck.

She was a furnace beneath his writhing body, one radiating intense heat as his fingers pulled at the loops of her skin-tight pants.

She turned her face away and spoke as he left a trail of kisses along her neck. "Let's move this party to the bed."

"*Mmmmm.*" His voice vibrated her throat.

He climbed off, black hair mussed, dick tugging so hard at the zipper of his jeans one could see every inch of his cock's drool-worthy outline. He scooped Aphrodite in his arms, coaxing a giddy giggle from her. Without strain, he swerved her around piles of clothes, guitars, and odd assortments of men's health magazines like someone deftly completing an obstacle course.

Barrett playfully tossed her onto the unmade queen-sized bed, and she laughed. But the heavenly sound halted the second Barrett peeled his black T-shirt off, exposing a hard-earned six-pack and a tapered deep 'V' of muscles that formed an arrow pointing straight to the crotch of his Wranglers.

She watched him undress, eyes studying his tanned deltoids and powerful biceps.

He smiled down, cocky, and unbuckled his belt, tugging it out of the loops in a flash. He folded it in his fists and pulled until it snapped like a crack of thunder.

Aphrodite jumped at the noise and rolled onto her stomach, watching him over her shoulder with a look of excitement mixed with fear.

"Does it turn you on, the thought of a naughty little Goddess getting the belt?"

She blushed, lying for a moment in silence.

Without even a trace of a smile, Barrett ran the folded belt softly over the meat of her ass, imagining the sexy pink mark it would leave on the skin beneath her jeans.

"It does… but I don't know the first thing about you. That sorta thing requires trust." She laid the side of her face on her clasped hands, bright hair spilling on the covers around her. "At least, for me."

Barrett studied her. He wished he'd learned to paint, wished he'd taken art seriously so that he could capture her beauty in this moment on a canvas. He'd hang it on his wall and stare at it for hours every day.

His face softened. He nodded and tossed the belt near a pile of rumpled laundry. "Fair enough."

Aphrodite rolled onto her back and yanked up on her shirt.

"No." He stopped her. "Half the fun on Christmas morning is unwrapping my presents. Don't you *dare* take that away from me."

She nodded and swallowed hard.

He pulled off her shirt slowly, marveling at her breasts from above, ones pouring out of her grape-purple bra.

"*Jesus*," he whispered, "*you really are a Goddess.*"

Barrett tugged her toward him until she was on the bed's edge. He moved her fingers to the waistband of his jeans. Her eyes stayed locked on his as she unbuttoned them. He could feel his pounding pulse throb in his dick, one that was dangerously close to that smart mouth of hers.

She pulled the zipper and peeled the jeans down his muscular legs, smiling at the eager bulge in his underwear. She leaned back onto her elbows as he stepped out of the lump of indigo material.

Barrett unbuttoned hers, ridding two curvaceous legs of all material, tossing the pants carelessly over his shoulder.

He glimpsed the large, graceful tattoo of a blue orchid that wound from her hip to her ribcage, tracing the edges of it with his finger softly.

Her legs parted, slow and with intent, offering him an unimpeded glance at the crotch of her soaked sapphire thong. He could tell through the thin material that her pussy was hairless. She was bare and beautiful beneath. His favorite. He feared his knees might buckle at the sight.

He leaned in and kissed her, deep and hard, reaching a hand beneath the underwire of her bra to cup the excited mound of flesh beneath. His eyes bolted open, and his head cocked to the side like a dog, a smile spreading across his shocked face.

"Pierced nipples?"

She nodded, sliding a hand down beneath the waistband of his underwear and grabbing a handful of his marble-hard ass.

"Goddamn, Aphrodite, now *that* is fuckin' *sexy*."

His thumb and forefinger teased the barbell, and she squirmed and smiled. He pried the cup of the bra up and drew the pink, studded bud into his mouth, playfully tonguing the metal. Every movement sent an unmistakable zing of pleasure through her, coaxing soft moans from her parted lips. It was music to Barrett's ears, a sensual, seductive tune he wanted to play on an endless loop.

He reached around and deftly sprung her bra loose in one quick motion.

"Wow. Done this before, have you?" she joked breathlessly, pulling her arms from the straps and tossing the constrictive article over her shoulder.

He shrugged. "Once or twice."

His mouth captured her other breast, and his torturous tongue flitted against the metal there, too. She hissed with pleasure.

Barrett kneeled on the bed, slipping between her thighs and forcing her back onto her elbows. He took a moment to appreciate the stunning creature beneath him, an image that blew every Victoria's Secret model he'd masturbated to as a boy right out of the water.

He traced a hand up and down her stomach, settling his fingertips in the waistband of her panties. She tilted her hips, and he peeled them off. Her thighs parted wide for him. She was wet and smooth, and his breath caught at the sight of her, naked on his sheets, his erection throbbing painfully against his boxer briefs.

He pressed his hips against hers, his fabric-covered cock resting against her warm entrance. She writhed as he slid against her. He savored the way each small thrust made her gasp a little.

With hooked thumbs, she snapped his waistband, startling him with the unexpected sensation. She giggled, and its sweet sound made something inside him wild.

He rolled her onto her stomach and wriggled out of his boxer briefs. He pried her legs apart with his knees and pressed his hard cock against her.

"One," she said.

"Excuse me?" He halted, still and throbbing.

"You can give me one... *little*... spanking," she muttered breathlessly.

Barrett smiled. "My, you are just *full* of surprises, aren't you?"

He caressed the soft skin of her ass and then slapped it with his palm, watching it jiggle beneath the stinging force. Aphrodite moaned into the fabric, bucking up toward him as if her body was begging for another.

"Is that all you got?" she moaned into the pillow.

Barrett scooped up her hips, pulling her up onto all fours. "Keep it up, Sweetheart, and I'll fuck the sass right out of you."

"*Promise*?" She wiggled her naked hips, pussy wet.

He grunted, moistened two fingers, and slid them deep inside of her.

She moaned, loud and long.

"You want me?" he growled.

She nodded.

"No, Aphrodite. You're gonna fucking say it with that pretty little mouth of yours. I *want* to hear you say, 'Please. Barrett, *fuck me.*'"

She didn't move. Didn't speak. She only smiled defiantly back at him.

He raised an eyebrow. "Is that so?"

He dipped his fingers into her again, sliding them all the way in without resistance. She groaned, nails digging into the comforter.

"You look beautiful like this, my fingers inside of you, pussy all wet and ready for me."

His cock raged at the sight of her arched back, at the warmth and wetness tightly enveloping his fingers.

"If you want my cock, you're gonna beg for it. You have to tell me how much you want it."

He hooked his fingers, pressing hard against the ridged flesh of her G-spot. Aphrodite rocked her hips back with need, fucking his hand, dragging them in and out of her as much as Barrett's wrist would allow.

"Barrett," she hissed, backing up against them again. "Please... *Fuck me.*"

He slipped his fingers out and gave her other ass cheek a hard spank, fingers leaving wet, pink marks where they made contact.

"Yes, Aphrodite, since you asked *nicely...*" He rose and shuffled to his dresser. Using his teeth, he tore open a condom wrapper and slipped the latex sheath around his engorged cock.

He strode back to the bed, yanked her by the hips back to the edge, forced her legs to spread wide, and pressed himself deep inside of her.

The instant he bottomed out, he groaned loudly, throwing his head back, savoring the feel of her pulsing, eager muscles as they clasped around him.

She shouted through the expansive loft, her pleasure echoing off the brick walls like a symphony. Every inch of him delved into her, seeking her most sensitive spots, the tilt of her hips silently guiding him to each.

They fucked as though they had both once been a single entity, one tragically separated, mending back into a perfect union of skin and bone. Every withdrawal from her warmth felt like a loss he would never recover from.

"Fuck! Just like that." Her lips dragged over her clenched fist as he hammered himself into her.

Her toes curled, muscles clenched, climactic wails sending shivers up Barrett's spine. The air hung heavy with their commingled scent as she screamed.

He gripped her hips so hard he imagined his clenched fingers leaving bruises, marks that would prove to other men that she was *his*, even if only for one night.

She pushed herself up, twisting, forcefully pulling him onto the bed. He fell to the blanket beside her, pliable and willing beneath her force. She climbed on top of him, sliding her trembling knees around his hips, sinking down onto him.

Barrett moaned as she leaned forward and rocked, nipping and licking at the perfect set of pierced breasts waved in his face.

She rocked her hips, sliding her clit against him, shamelessly using his body to procure another powerful orgasm for herself.

Barrett's hands roamed, grasping her ass, her hips, her breasts. She threw her head back in another loud orgasm, and his mouth split into a wicked grin. As she tightened around him, he released his own torrent of pleasure, dick pulsing, jaw tight as he came inside of her.

After a long moment of silence, she collapsed forward, burying her face in the crook of his sweaty neck, content body melted and weak.

He kissed her softly, nuzzling her nose, hands playing with her colorful tresses.

She flopped down to the bed with a smile, and they both lay side-by-side in the silence, staring at the ceiling.

"I know you said you don't do sleepovers, but that was a damn-near religious experience, and I'm not ready to let you go after just one round."

She smiled and rested her face on his chest, closing her eyes to enjoy the sensation of his rough hands as they stroked her naked skin.

3

Bvvvvvvvvvrrrrrrrrrrrr.

The sound of the phone's vibrations awoke them.

"You need to get that?"

He looked at the caller ID and flopped the phone back down. "Ugh. Let it ring," he grumbled.

Bvvvvvvvvvrrrrrrrrrrrr.

He turned and grasped her bare hips, pulling her close. She wrapped a leg around his waist, feeling his half-hard shaft graze the area between her thighs. Her lips found his in the darkness, his tongue seeking the wet comforts of her mouth.

Barrett grabbed her bare ass and swatted it with a playful *thwap*.

Bvvvvvvvvvrrrrrrrrrrrr.

As their kiss deepened, her hands wandered, tracing his biceps with her fingertips. "Who would call you this late?"

He traced one of her breasts with an index finger.

Her body stiffened. "You should pick up. It could be important."

He nodded, catching her lower lip with his teeth and giving it a rough nibble.

Bvvvvvvvvvrrrrrrrrrrr.

The sound doused him with a cold wave of reality. He crawled out of the bed with an apologetic look.

"Don't... move."

She watched pale moonlight paint the edges of his firm ass and muscular thighs.

Snatching his cell phone from somewhere on the floor, the screen lit up his strong jawline. He slammed his finger against the answer button and spoke. "What?" The voice on the other end sounded angry. "You're right. I'm sorry. It's just late," he said, glancing at his phone to see the time. "Or super early, I guess. Did you sleep at all?"

A woman's voice seeped through the other end. Aphrodite sat up, covering her tits with a thin sheet.

"No," he mumbled, "It's okay. Did you need something?"

There was a pause, and his shoulders visibly sagged. He rubbed the bridge of his nose in frustration. "You want *me* to go?"

Her smile fell with the sudden realization that Barrett might be attached. His being in a relationship had never even occurred to her.

She'd never even asked. She barely knew anything about him.

She searched for her bra and panties in the dark, eavesdropping.

Who was on the phone with him? Another booty call?

A girlfriend?

A wife?

She glanced around the apartment. Even in the moonlit darkness, there wasn't a feminine touch to be found. No throw pillows. No candles. No blankets hanging from the couch. Not a hint of perfume or women's clothes in the floor piles. There wasn't one piece of wall art with positive affirmations or a single meaningless decoration on his coffee table.

"Of *course* he does." Barrett grimaced, hanging his head in defeat. "Alright! Fine! I'll lay off. Just sayin' that of the two of us, I got the brains *and* the brawn, and Dusty got nothin' but a weak spine."

Dusty?

"Yeah, I'll take you. What time am I picking you up?"

He threw his head back, exasperated. "*Seven?!* Can we go to a later service?"

Service?

Oh, God.

Aphrodite felt a chill run through her as she clasped her bra. She hurriedly put on her underwear inside-out and searched for the rest of her clothes.

"I'm just saying, you don't always have to go to the early one just because Susan's there. It's not high school. I promise you get the same amount of talking snakes and pestilence at the later service, too."

In less than a minute, Aphrodite was dressed and creeping toward the front door.

Barrett silently waved her away from it.

She pointed to it and mouthed, '*I'm gonna go.*'

"No," he whispered, holding up a finger for Aphrodite to wait. "Fine, Gam-Gam. I gotta go. I'll see you… in," he looked at his watch, "three hours."

Aphrodite exhaled hard.

Gam-Gam?

That certainly didn't seem like the kind of pet name for a lover.

"Alright, Grandma. No problem. I love you, too."

He pressed the 'end call' button, tired eyes turning back to the woman in his doorway. "Jesus Christ. Sorry about that. She doesn't sleep much ever since my grandfather died. I think she forgets the rest of us *do* sleep sometimes."

"That's okay. I should go."

"No," he said, quiet and firm, approaching her.

Her eyes studied his nude body, feet frozen in place like her shoes were made of concrete.

He pressed her against the door slowly, teasing her with lips held an inch away. "You should stay."

She tilted her chin up, tongue aching to taste him once more before the nagging question burst from her throat. "What church do you attend?"

He studied her for a moment. "She goes to New Hope. I go, too, sometimes. You know, when her ride shits out."

She swallowed so hard Barrett could feel it in his own body.

"Why? What about you?"

"I'm... not big on church," she lied.

He traced her bottom lip with his finger and leaned in closer. "So why are we wasting precious time talking about it?"

"You have to get up in a few hours, and so do I. We should try to get some sleep."

Barrett pulled his hands away and offered her space. "Yeah. Fine. You might be right."

She took a deep breath and opened the door a crack.

"Wait a second, Cinderella." He unlocked his phone and handed it to her. "Can I at least get your number? I'd like to do this again sometime."

She grabbed his cell quickly and entered a number and the name *Aphrodite* before handing it back.

"Maybe I'll call, and sometime you'll let me take you out on a proper date."

"We'll see." She rose on her toes and kissed him softly on the lips. "G'night, Barrett."

"Night, Aphrodite."

He lingered at the open door, even after she was out of sight, before finally closing it.

4

The cluster of congregants shuffled their way out of the early service of the New Hope Church. Churchgoers mobbed the exit slowly, eager to get to mid-morning brunches. The mass of clustered bodies made Barrett feel claustrophobic.

His grandmother clung to his arm, walking molasses-slow up the aisle as they funneled toward Pastor Erikson and his wife, Maggie, who stood at the exit shaking everyone's hands in the name of fellowship.

"Stella," crooned a fragile voice from a row in the middle of the church.

Barrett rolled his eyes at the sound of Susan's voice. Susan Glenecky was an annoying gossip Barrett had the misfortune of knowing most of his life due to her miraculously befriending his saint of a grandmother. Even though every sermon was only an hour long, it was nearly two hours before Barrett could take Gam-Gam home with all the catching up Susan usually had to do. As soon as the motor-mouth had caught sight of his grandmother, it was game over.

Susan hobbled over to Stella and gave her a hug. As they embraced, Barrett wondered if either of them ever remembered a time when a telephone didn't exist. They certainly seemed old enough. Susan looked like if you touched her, she would crumble like cheap plaster.

"My gosh, son," Susan grabbed Barrett's forearm and squeezed, "You look more like your father every day."

"Thanks, Mrs. Glenecky. You look extra... *purple* today, by the way." Barrett gestured to her gaudy outfit, trying to make it sound like a compliment. The woman looked like a shriveled eggplant.

"Thank you!" Susan attempted a brittle curtsy and showcased her top row of dentures in a smile akin to a Chihuahua's growl. "You look dashing as well. I love the tie."

Barrett readjusted the Windsor knot of his necktie, one a hideous brown, dotted with repeating donuts and sprinkles. "Thanks. Gam-Gam bought it for me."

"I figured as much. You look like you haven't eaten a donut since you were a little boy. Oh, gosh, what adorably chubby cheeks you used to have!" She reached out to pinch his cheek, and Barrett artfully dodged. The old coot's age-spotted hands had a grip like a vice.

The crowd further congealed as everyone jammed into the main aisle. People huffed as they tried to exit, having already forgotten about the patience preached about in the sermon.

Barrett held Stella's hand, and Susan chattered about the week's goings-on. Barrett escorted them toward the pastor with an arm around each to corral them. He could see the snow-dusted lawn up ahead through the open doors. They were in the home stretch.

"Are you listening to me, Barrett?" Susan asked, clutching his wrist hard as an icy breeze blasted in and ruffled through her short blue-gray ringlets.

Mentally, Barrett had been miles away, reminiscing about the rainbow-haired vixen on her knees, draped over his bedspread, begging him to fuck her just a few short hours before.

"Hmmm?"

"I said I have a girl I want you to meet," Susan exclaimed as if it were headline news.

"Oh, God." He groaned. "Susan, we agreed. No more blind dates. I refuse."

"I know, I know, but she just got back from college. Plus, she's the pastor's daughter, so you know she's not a trollop."

Stella elbowed Susan in the side.

"Ow! What?!"

"Watch your language. We are in a church!"

"Lord almighty, Stella, it's not like I said '*hussy*,'" Susan growled, rubbing her side.

Barrett tried to wrangle them past the pastor. Susan snatched the pastor's wife by the arm and pulled her in for a kiss on the cheek with her bizarre old woman strength. "Maggie! Good to see you! You remember Barrett."

Maggie stretched out an arm, white gown with tulip sleeves swaying as she reached for his hand. Her deceptively youthful eyes were bright, face framed with gentle curls of sandy-blonde hair.

Damn, he thought. *If she were a decade younger and unattached...*

Maybe.

"Barrett! How are you?" Maggie's voice was soft and comforting, but there was something disingenuous about it that he couldn't quite put his finger on.

"Pleasure to see you again, Mrs. Erikson," Barrett kept his tone reverent and shook her hand.

Pastor Erikson straightened his bulky frame and shook Barrett's hand next, squeezing it so hard that Barrett nearly yelped.

"Pastor. Good to see you again. Heck of a grip you got there."

"That Bible ain't *light,* you know!" The pastor laughed. "Good to see you, son. It's been a while. How'd you like the sermon?"

Susan's eyes drifted to the pastor's wrist, stuck on the wrinkled cuff of his suit jacket.

"Great. Felt like just what I needed to hear today," Barrett lied.

"Glad to hear it. We could all use a little more patience these days."

Susan leaned closer to Maggie and whispered loud enough for the others to hear. "Your husband is all wrinkled. You need to borrow my iron? It wouldn't be any trouble. It has the steam bit and everything."

Maggie flashed a look of embarrassment. "I… have an iron."

The pastor looked at the crinkled fabric and rocked on his feet. "More pressing things in life have been occupying our time as of late, I'm afraid."

Maggie jumped in. "I've been so busy leading the women's Bible study groups and working on the new children's Sunday school sermons. Plus, I've been coordinating a drive to collect meals and coats for the less fortunate."

"Well, Barrett could help with all of your ironing." Susan grinned. "He's a *maid* now. Can you believe it?"

Barrett swallowed hard, his ugly tie suddenly seeming far too tight. "My job is more janitorial than anything."

Last week, he'd told his grandmother about quitting his old job hauling furniture to start a new job at *Man Maid*, Jackson Hole's all-male cleaning service. Of course, he did so in the *broadest* of strokes. He told her that they catered to a very particular niche clientele. He told her about the Halloween costumes and said that most of his clients would be rich, bored housewives who wanted both *a cheap thrill and a clean grill*.

Stella was open-minded and no stranger to Barrett's antics through the years. She loved him for exactly the man he was, and her acceptance of his wild shenanigans through the years only strengthened their bond. Hearing that he had joined a nearly nude cleaning service only shocked Stella because her grandson seemed painfully *under*qualified for the cleaning part, having seen the condition of his bachelor pad worsen over the last decade.

But hearing this news from Susan's lips made Barrett wonder how much Stella had actually told the old chatterbox. Did she think he was just a regular run-of-the-mill house cleaner? Or had Gam-Gam divulged *all* of the dirty details?

"Really? I've never actually heard of a man being a maid, funny enough." Maggie chuckled. "That's so… *interesting.*"

"Yep." Barrett pursed his lips for a moment. "I clean homes, do laundry, power-wash concrete… you name it." He waved her off. "But I'm sure you have everything under control. Asking a maid to come in… seems like overkill."

"No! Actually, this is perfect timing," the pastor said.

"Maybe we could use your services now that I'm trying to juggle all of this stuff. Plus, our daughter just moved back home, and she's a bit of a… a *disaster.*" The last word soured Maggie's face, and she stared at the carpet.

Pastor Erikson scoffed. "She's a tornado. Gets it from her mother."

Maggie flashed an irritated glare at him.

"I'm kidding, of course." The pastor threw a beefy arm around his wife's shoulder. "You're an angel, off sharing your light with as many people as you can. There's nothing wrong with that. I could just as easily pick up the iron if I wasn't doing the same."

Maggie forced her mouth up into a weak smile. "I'm not sure we could afford your services, unfortunately."

"Oh, I'm sure he'd do it free of charge," Susan offered, nudging Barrett. "Anything for the Lord. Right, Barrett?"

"Oh, gosh, no. We'd pay you, of course," Maggie said quietly.

"Nonsense," Stella crowed, her kind eyes suddenly pleading with Barrett to do it as a favor to her.

Barrett sighed, "Of course. Anything for the Lord."

But he wasn't offering for the Lord. It was Stella that weakened him. His Gam-Gam had sacrificed so much over the years for his comfort. She asked for so little. A few hours of volunteer work felt like the least he could do to repay her.

Pastor Erikson swatted Barrett hard. "When can you start?"

"Let me get with my new boss and check my work schedule."

"Do you have a business card?" Maggie asked.

"No, not yet."

Grabbing a pen and a program from the morning's sermon out of her giant purse, Susan offered them to Barrett. "Here. Write down your phone number so they can call you."

"Thanks, Susan. You're so... *helpful* today," Barrett said through gritted teeth, hurriedly jotting down his digits, hoping his messy handwriting would be too difficult to decipher.

He handed it to Maggie and smiled. "Hopefully, it'll work out."

Another untruth. *How many times would he be forced to lie in God's house in one morning?*

"Perfect." The pastor waved at a cluster of stragglers approaching from behind. "If you'll excuse me, I have to discuss some things about the new children's wing with these fine folks. Lovely seeing you all."

As Barrett's dress shoes crunched halfway across the dead grass, he whipped around to Susan and glared. In a half-scream-half-whisper, he growled, *"What was that*?!"

"What?" Susan shrugged, oblivious. "It's a client, ain't it? You're welcome!"

5

Chastity's rainbow-striped hair was a matted mess against her pillow. The faint memory of all that had been done to tangle it the night before brought a smile to her sleepy face.

Her body ached, remembering the stranger from the bar she'd gone home with, the man with abs you could scrub a load of laundry on. The man with the perfect jawline and the effortless tan who knew the perfect way to curl his fingers to get her to scream his name.

She remembered the faint taste of bourbon on his tongue, the feel of his calloused fingers manipulating her barbells, the sharp sting of his spankings...

She sat up and grabbed her laptop, wiping sleep from her eyes as it booted. Moments later, her fingertips hammered away at the keys, mind whirling with questions.

Now that she wasn't in college, could she stay here in Jackson Hole, where so many people knew she was an Erikson?

Could she start fresh somewhere new, somewhere no one suspected she was a pastor's daughter?

At the sound of the door opening, she tore her eyes away from the screen. The door cracked a few inches, and her mother silhouetted in the searing beam of light pouring in from the hall. Chastity looked at the time and grimaced.

1:03 p.m.

Fuck.

"Chastity? Honey, are you decent?" Maggie asked through the crack.

Chastity set the laptop aside. "Debatable."

Maggie stepped in and smoothed her dress. "Honey, your father and I heard you sneak in at four in the morning. Got a great shot of you doing it on the Ring camera, too, in case you would like to try to deny it."

"No need." Chastity shrugged. "I thought I was an adult. I didn't realize I had an imposed curfew."

"You do. Same as before you went off to college." Maggie stood in silence for a moment. "You must've been exhausted, seeing how you slept through both of today's services."

Chastity snorted and wiped her eye with the heel of her hand, smearing last night's eye makeup to her temple. "Oh darn. Did I miss another 'pray away the gay' sermon? Or was

58

Dad too busy telling horny teenagers to practice celibacy? Newsflash: kids in junior high are banging each other like bunnies."

Maggie cocked her hip. "Stop talking about *banging*."

"Speaking of *banging*," Chastity mocked, adding more emphasis to the word than needed, "You just walked in like that? What if I had a guy in here? Or better yet, a *girl*."

Pinching her eyes closed, trying to block out the mental picture her daughter had just gifted her, Maggie sneered, "Why do you say things like that? To upset me? Look around you, Chastity."

Chastity scanned her messy room. Across from her bed were several shelves crowded with cluttered piles of books. All around them were medals, trophies, and framed awards, some for sports, others for clubs, Dean's Lists, Honor Roll...

An animal encyclopedia sat on her nightstand, an award ribbon tucked inside to hold her place.

"Well, what do you see?" Maggie asked sharply.

With brutal honesty and a hint of sarcasm, Chastity shrugged. "An overachiever with a low self-esteem? A try-hard? A perfectionist burnout?

Or were you looking for just one word? If so, the word is *sad*."

Maggie probed her tongue against her cheek. "Sad? What do you have to be sad about?"

Chastity rolled her eyes and snatched up her laptop, returning her focus to the screen. "You're right, Mother. You're *always* right. Consider me one of God's greatest tribulations for you. You know how He just loves to give people challenges. Poor you. Go commiserate with your buddy, Job."

"When you're done with your little pity party, and you're ready to join the rest of civilized society, feel free to join us for our prayer meeting in the study."

"Hard pass," Chastity grumbled, scrolling through a search of available apartments.

Clenching her jaw, Maggie gripped the handle on the door. "I love you, Sweetheart, even if you are hellbent on making that as difficult as possible."

She dragged the door closed. Chastity fumed in silence. She wanted to be in a different *world*. One less complicated and demanding.

She was ready to minimize the search, ready to escape into some trash reality TV show where the biggest problems people had were *which SPF to wear sunbathing*, but her fingers paused, and her eyes scanned the listing for a luxury apartment -- one she couldn't afford -- on the opposite side of town. She wasn't sure how she would make rent in such an expensive town, but staying in her childhood bedroom was not a viable option. Even if it seemed unattainable, she had to find a way to escape.

6

The morning's chill nipped at Barrett's bare biceps as he marched up the icy walkway of Mrs. Thompson's sprawling ranch-style mansion, one located on twenty-four acres of land on the outskirts of the mountainous town. His hands batted against the camouflage design on his Army combat pants. His heartbeat thundered beneath his matching shirt, unbuttoned to reveal a sliver of tanned muscles. He swallowed hard and stared at the doorbell camera.

He was being recorded. Somewhere in the cloud was now an image of his oiled abs peeking out from a tactical work shirt, feet nervously tensed in slightly undersized surplus store combat boots. He had been asked to come as a horny soldier on leave, ready for a different kind of action.

It'll get easier, he chanted, echoing Will Jessup's words during his first morning briefing. Soon, this would all be second nature, but today, his nerves felt like a teen stripped to his underwear in the middle of a pep rally.

Could be worse, he remembered Will saying. *You could be in a soul-sucking cubicle listening to coworkers repeat the same dull stories.*

Before he could knock, a woman in her late fifties threw open the door. Her forehead warred with a month-old dose of Botox in its attempt to crease with surprise. Collagen-plumped lips slathered in berry-colored lipstick gaped in shock.

"Hello, ma'am. First Lieutenant Bulge, reporting for duty." He clicked his heels together and saluted aggressively, trying his best to remember how they did it in movies like *Platoon* and *Apocalypse Now*.

"At ease, soldier." She grinned. "Follow me."

Bolt-upright, he clasped his arms behind his back and followed her in, whistling as he entered the grand foyer.

So much glass. So much marble. So many shining surfaces.

This was going to be a pain in the ass.

"My, they never seem to disappoint at *Man Maid*, do they?" Mrs. Thompson's stiletto Louis Vuitton heels traipsed toward him, arms extended for his jacket. He stripped it off with a smile and handed it to her, pumping his bare pecs as she turned away to hang it on a coat rack.

Her gaze raked down his sculpted body, settling on the lump in the front of his pants. "I see why they call you Lieutenant Bulge."

She shook her head to regain her composure and returned her eyes to his face. "Alright, let me show you to the laundry room. My normal housemaid just had a baby and is on maternity leave for a few weeks. I'll have you come in her stead a few times a week while she's away. The poor thing's water broke all over my Ernesta Sugar rug. Then, she used my seven-hundred-dollar imported *towels* to clean it up, if you can believe it. I was just *sick* over it. I'd have tossed them, but Will said you guys are great with laundry. Clean them up so I can gift them to her. I'm sure they're nicer than anything she'll ever be able to afford."

Mrs. Thompson strutted down the corridor. Barrett followed, taking the opportunity to appreciate every bit of the tight figure beneath her clinging silk dress. He half-listened as she droned on, fantasizing about what her bare ass might look like and if she'd be a voracious cougar type in bed. It was women like her, in his experience, who let loose the most between the sheets.

…Except for *Aphrodite*.

The sudden recollection of her pierced nipples in his fingers hardened him. He cleared his throat and tried to focus on whatever Mrs. Thompson was blathering on about.

They turned the corner into a laundry room nearly as spacious as his loft apartment. He stomped in ahead of her, giving her a gorgeous view of his muscular back and marble-hard butt. He looked at a floor-to-ceiling wall of chemical detergents between two massive windows. Bizarre cleaning tools on an eye-level shelf reminded him of the torture instruments he'd once seen in an action movie.

Lining both side walls were large washing machines and dryers, neither of which he was confident he knew how to operate.

You're thirty-four years old, Barrett. You know how to clean by now. And if you don't know how to do something, hell, fake it 'til you make it. Just make sure you look damn hot while you're doin' it, Will had said.

"So," he muttered smoothly, twisting in his too-tight boots to face her, "this is where you want me to start?"

"I don't think I *stuttered*." She folded her arms.

"What about… the *bedroom*?" He stepped closer. "Sure you don't want me to start there?"

She studied him for a moment, stunned by the brazen proposition to lay her only moments after gaining entry to her home. She toyed with her wedding band, one studded with enough diamonds that its glittery surface could be seen in Idaho. "I'm married, Romeo. To a man who gives me all of this." She gestured to her opulent surroundings. "Keep it in your fatigues, Officer Bulge, and get started on those towels."

It was worth a shot, he thought. *Any activity would beat actually having to clean.*

Barrett nodded, saluted her again, and turned toward the several baskets of laundry nestled in the corner. Banging the cougar would have been so much easier than stain-treating placenta-covered towels…

Or *whatever the hell* was on them.

***

Exhausted by several hours of work, Barrett tossed the scrub sponge in the bottom of the huge Jacuzzi in the master bath, cranked the water to cold, and dunked his head beneath the faucet.

In the doorway, Mrs. Thompson tapped her manicured nails on the jamb and smiled. "Mmmm. Working up a sweat?"

He turned off the faucet and nodded, flinging beads of water into the bottom of the tub. His muscles rippled, flexing as he stood. He shook his short hair like a dog, speckling the heated mirror beside the bath.

"Is today… your first day on the job?"

"Yeah, it is. How'd you know?" He wiped his hands on her crisp, white Egyptian cotton bathrobe and then scrubbed his face with a towel on the chrome bar above the Jacuzzi, leaving it crooked.

Mrs. Thompson just stared at him with a look of displeasure.

He followed her gaze to the towel and realized his mistake. He straightened it on the bar, backing away when he seemed satisfied.

Sue rolled her eyes. "Well, Colonel Boner—"

"First Lieutenant Bulge, ma'am," he corrected, standing at attention and saluting her again.

"At ease, soldier." She motioned to him with flattened hands. "I think that'll be all. Your tour of duty just ended."

He looked inside the tub at the line of shaved hair and soap residue he hadn't yet finished scrubbing. "Yes, ma'am."

He nodded, feeling panic wad in his chest. She had scheduled him for five hours. It hadn't even been three since he knocked on her front door. Either she got what she wanted:

An eyeful and a moderately cheap thrill…

Or she was displeased entirely.

They hadn't even gotten to the part where he shed his fatigues and scrubbed tile grout in his small "*Be all you can be*" banana hammock yet.

"Ma'am, if you don't mind, I'd like to at *least* finish folding the laundry. You paid for five hours."

He shuddered to think about the painful look of disappointment he'd have to see in Will's eyes if his first client was disgruntled.

"I'll get everything folded and hung up before I leave, so nothing'll be wrinkled for you."

She nodded and followed him out, but not before catching a glimpse of the dirty sponge he'd left in the half-scrubbed bath. She shook her head.

A few minutes later, as she rounded the doorway into the laundry room, she stopped, frozen in horror as the faux-soldier pulled an armful of fluff-covered fabric out of the dryer.

"Oh, dear God…" Barrett grimaced, thoroughly embarrassed at the presence of the powder-blue fibers on every inch of the load in his grasp. A mostly disintegrated bath rug dangled from the mouth of the machine.

Mrs. Thompson covered her mouth to stifle a scream, her lifted face flashing angrily scarlet. "What did you *do*? You… fucking *moron*?!"

"Moron?!" Barrett froze. "Your frickin'… *bath mat* self-destructed like a bomb!"

She stormed over and snatched the remains of the rug. She flicked the little white tag dangling from the shred that remained. "Did you read the instructions?!"

"I shouldn't have to! It's a rug!"

"You. Don't. Wash. A. Rug. With. Delicate. Expensive. Fabrics!" She snapped, slapping her palms with each word. She tossed the destroyed rug on the floor and yanked the items in his hands out in a burst of anger.

"Hey, lady, those were clean!"

"Those are *covered* in rug fibers!"

"So is your *floor*, now!" Barrett growled in frustration.

Staring down at the mound of fabric, she cocked her head sideways and lifted a towel from the pile. She held it up, staring at Barrett through a fist-sized hole melted through the middle of it.

"What... the...?"

"Oh shit." Barrett swallowed, Adam's apple bouncing hard in his throat. "I might have used too much bleach."

Mrs. Thompson glowered at him, lowering the towels and rolling her shoulders back. She looked like a bulldog, forcing an under-bite.

"They were white towels! You told me to remove the gunk, so I stain-treated them!"

"You poured bleach straight onto a seven-hundred dollar towel?! Jesus, I thought it was your first day on the *job*. I didn't realize it was your first day ever cleaning in your *life*!"

"Now, Mrs. Thompson, there's no need to be cruel... I'll just... *replace* them."

"Replace them?" She laughed cruelly. "You're going to go to *Italy* and get me replacement towels?"

"Well, no. But Target has some nice—"

"Target?! *Target?!*" She looked like she might pass out. She shot a finger toward the door. "Get the hell out of my house, Lieutenant *Imbecile*!"

7

Barrett glanced around the *Man Maid* office
in an uncomfortable leather armchair. With a few
coats of paint and Will's life savings, the
downtown building had been transformed from
the stale remains of a raided massage parlor to a
new, sleek, modern storefront. Silver metal lined
the windows, previously-broken ones Ava had
replaced immediately. Once-beige walls were
now a breathtaking teal damask wallpaper
accented with crown molding and all-new
baseboards. The room smelled of lavender
essential oils. Soothing classical music played
quietly through hidden speakers, furthering the
small establishment's posh feel.

A large glass desk, one Will and Barrett
dragged over from Ava's prior home office, sat
in the middle. A minibar stocked with bottles of
Fiji and seltzer water was next to it, labels all
facing out.

Behind the desk hung a horizontal canvas
print covering most of the back wall. It was an
image of a shirtless Will Jessup holding a spray
bottle in bright yellow rubber gloves. It was a

smaller copy of the same billboards that now peppered Highway 191 near the affluent neighborhoods.

The glass front door opened, and a waft of men's cologne -- sweat and cedar with a hint of citrus -- flooded Barrett's nostrils.

He chuckled, knowing who it was before he even turned. "'Sup, you dink?"

But Will wasn't laughing. His face was contorted in a grim expression of anger, something Barrett had rarely seen in decades of knowing him.

He'd fucked up. That was clear.

Will slapped Barrett on the back of the head. *Hard.*

"Ow! You dick!"

Ava entered with an armful of binders and a stony stare. She slapped Barrett in the back of the head, too.

"Alright!" Barrett rubbed the sore spot where her engagement ring cracked against his scalp. "Use your freakin' *words*, people!"

Ava sat in the chair at the desk, her black blazer and skirt making her look every bit the fierce businesswoman she was. Will stood beside her in sweaty gym clothes, staring at Barrett.

"I just have one question," Will muttered.

"What's that?" Barrett struggled to make eye contact.

"What… the *fuck*, dude?!"

"What?" Barrett shrugged, trying to downplay his disastrous afternoon. He jostled his camo-clad knees nervously. "The hiccup at Mrs. Thompson's? So I murdered some broad's bathroom rug and put a hole in a towel. Big deal. That ain't even *close* to grounds for not *one* but *two* head slaps."

"Hiccup? This wasn't a hiccup, Barrett! Thompson was a regular client! I've been cleaning her place for almost a year now. She pays on time and tips *gen-er-ous-ly*. This was a huge account!"

"Some chick already gave *birth* on those towels, or whatever! They were *already* ruined with afterbirth… or placenta… or whatever-the-fuck *goo* comes out of a woman when she calves out!"

Ava leaned back and bit her tongue, looking out the glass front door at the traffic outside.

"Besides the rug and the towels, she said you did sub-par work on the kitchen and the bathroom. And, probably worse than all of that, she said you *propositioned* her. Said you asked her right off the bat if she wouldn't rather start in the *bedroom*. Sue said you came onto her."

"Hey, isn't that what this is all about? Servicing horny old women while their husbands are at work or some shit? Or am I just... misunderstanding."

"You're *misunderstanding!*" Ava yelled, her voice booming powerfully in the small room.

"Wow. I'm at a loss for words," Will said, hugging his damp chest with glistening, ripped arms.

"Dude, come on! It was my first day! I'll get 'em next time," Barrett said casually.

Ava shook her head.

"*There won't be a next time,*" Will spoke quietly. "We gotta let you go, Bud."

Barrett swallowed the lump in his throat. "What? No. Over a *rug*? That's what insurance is for. Take it out of my pay or something. Don't fuckin' *fire* me."

Ava growled, "You tried to *sleep* with her! You left the house in more of a mess than when you arrived! *Then,* you fucked up her dryer with the rug. It wasn't a cheap one *either*, Barrett. It was *industrial*. And apparently, her towels and rug were worth more than my first fucking *Honda*." She moaned and rubbed her eyes. "Now our insurance is gonna take a hit."

"With the repairs and replacements, you just put us in the red this month for the first time since I started this business. Look around you, Barrett. I'm not running this place out of my pickup truck as a side hustle now. This is a real business. One with a very *particular* clientele. Rich women, Barrett... they *talk*."

"One negative review takes about ten positive ones just to equal out," Ava said, chiming in. "Plus, we can't have you jeopardizing us *legally*, either."

"Ugh, what the fuck are you even talking about?" Barrett flopped his head backward.

"Hey, that's my future *wife* you're talking to right now, *and* your *boss*—"

"For another, what, thirty-nine seconds?!" Barrett threw his hands up and let them flop on the overstuffed arms of the chair with a *thunk*.

"I don't care if you're my best friend or not. You can talk to *me* how you please, but you *will* show *her* some goddamned *respect*."

"Fine. I'm sorry, Ava," Barrett grumbled. Ava didn't acknowledge him.

Will continued. "Thompson is a paying client. If you'd have slept with her, that's called *prostitution*. It's illegal. This isn't Vegas. You don't work at the *Bunny Ranch*. You even offering made her uncomfortable. A major part of this business we are trying to build relies on female safety and *empowerment*. These clients, *they're* the ones in control. Not us. I've seen her. If Thompson wanted to get laid, she could go to half the bars in this town and pick up a horny knucklehead that she can dose with her husband's *Viagra*."

Ava interjected. "You're not the only six-pack in town, Barrett. We've got a line of guys from *Swole* who want to join the fleet and have a lot more domestic experience than you. This was a favor to Will, bringing you on."

Barrett stared at Will like he was Judas Iscariot from one of Pastor Erikson's New Testament sermons. "Cleaning isn't that complicated, guys. You don't need some kind of a degree to be a fucking *janitor in hot pants*."

"Says the man whose apartment hasn't been clean since the Bush administration," Will said with a scoff.

"*Senior*, not '*W*,'" Ava added.

Will gave her a look that begged for her to let him handle it. "Ava will cut you your first and final check. I'm sorry this didn't work out."

"Wow." Barrett laughed. "Guess this means I'm no longer your Best Man, either."

Will shook his head. "No. Business and family are separate. You're still my friend. Still my Best Man. I love you like a brother, Barrett. I just… can't risk everything *we've* worked so hard to build on someone who can't take this seriously."

Barrett ran his hands through his thick quiff of black hair, stood, and turned toward the door.

"Sorry that I let you down." Barrett put his hand on the glass. "*Both* of you."

Ava nodded, averting her gaze.

"Wanna shoot some pool tonight?" Will tried to soften the blow.

"Rain-check, maybe." Barrett shook his head and stepped out.

After a long moment of silence, Ava finally muttered the word, "Fuck."

"What?" Will rubbed the top of her back.

"Dammit!"

"You having a sudden change of heart?"

Ava nodded. "Go grab him, would you?"

Will nodded and raced out of the building. He hollered for Barrett and waved him back in.

"What?" Barrett looked like a whipped puppy as he re-entered, shoulders sunken. "You wanna just give me my final check now to save postage or somethin'?"

Ava sighed deeply.

"If it's about the wedding, the answer is 'no.' I haven't gotten my tux fitted yet."

"Seriously? You have to order ahead. I said that in my email last month when I sent you all the information."

Will chimed in. "Please, Barrett, just… get fitted." His eyes flashed his friend a glance that said: *Don't test her. She's serious. I'm scared. Please send help.*

Ava finally spoke with reluctance. "We'll give you another shot. You're on probation."

Barrett smiled. "Isn't the *first* time. Surely, it won't be the last."

Will smirked. "Not something to brag about, Mr. Bar-Room-Brawler."

"As I was saying," Ava looked back and forth at the men, "being that you're Will's best friend, it feels like it would be... *prudent*... to give you another shot. I suppose we are a little to blame since we never provided you with any formal training."

"We assumed you'd know how to wash towels. That was *our* bad," Will said sarcastically.

"We should have tried to teach you or had someone teach you right off the bat. We're growing, and this is opening my eyes to a deficiency on our end. I obviously don't have any knowledgeable staff to train you other than Will, but we'll hire someone soon. In the meantime, if you want to stay on board, you need to be proactive in finding yourself some training. I don't mean just cleaning up that pit you call an apartment, either. Will can type up a list of tips and tricks of the trade he's picked up."

"Sure," he said, agreeing quickly.

"In the meantime, Barrett, watch some *YouTube* videos. Learn a thing or two about laundry and mixing cleaning chemicals so you don't end up *mustard-gassing* yourself unconscious or burning more holes in Italian imported towels. *Capiche?*"

"Hearing the sentencing loud and clear, Your Honor." Barrett bowed.

"Starla and I barely see Will as it is these days. It's the reason we hired you. So, I'll still need you to find some outside sources for information while I compile a training course for new hires."

"Yeah, I get it." Barrett nodded and smiled a little at Will. "Gam-Gam's friend, Susan—"

"Ugh." Will couldn't help but make a disgusted noise at the sound of Susan's name.

"I know. Right?" Barrett chuckled. "She blabbed to the pastor's wife at our church that I was a maid. Not," he injected quickly, "one that does it in my *briefs*, mind you. She thinks I'm just a regular old housekeeper-type maid."

Will laughed and covered his face, trying to compose himself. "Of course she did. That woman's got a mouth the size 'a Texas, I swear."

"Well, she volunteered me to come to Maggie's and clean. Might be a good chance to practice a little. At least this way, if I fuck up, it's not your company at stake."

Ava's face brightened, and she rose from her seat. She made her way to Barrett and wrapped her arms around him. "I'm sorry, Barrett. I know you're trying."

He hugged her back, and Will's rosy cheeks rose at the sight of it.

"We are just at a critical point here," she continued. "Feels like one wrong move, and we could lose everything. Everything's riding on this, Barrett."

"I know." He squeezed her tighter. "I'll do better. I promise."

"I know you will."

"Where's a camera when I need one? This is a real Hallmark moment," Will jested.

Barrett's middle finger rose behind Ava's back.

Ava playfully shoved Barrett backward by the shoulder. "You're like a little brother to me. Sometimes little brothers piss you off."

Barrett grabbed a fistful of Ava's blonde hair and yanked.

"Ow!"

"Sometimes little brothers do shit like that, too." Barrett laughed, then smiled. "Wow... I'm impressed. That was your *real* hair. I always assumed those were extensions."

Ava smacked him in the chest a little harder than she intended. "Get the fuck out. Go. Go learn how to do stuff that twelve-year-old little boys already *know* how to do." She smiled.

"Yeah," Barrett started out the door again, "Love you, too, sis."

8

Another night.

Another bar.

Another free drink bought by a horny rig worker.

It's amazing what an arm graze and a sweet laugh'll getcha these days, Chastity thought as she chugged half of the ice-cold beer the bartender had just shoved her way. She wiped her mouth on the back of her hand and clicked glasses with the mediocre-looking roughneck who bought it for her.

He wouldn't be half bad…

If he had all his teeth.

Chastity rolled her neck and sighed loudly. Despite her agitation at the day's events and the barrage of non-stop chatter, she had missed *The Alibi*, her old run-down haunt. The place felt like it hadn't aged a day in the years she'd been gone. It felt a little like *home*, more so than her *real* one.

She recalled how much she used to love sneaking in when she was underage. The staff all knew her by name and couldn't have cared less about checking her license.

The town was small. They knew who she was and took pity on her for being the pastor's daughter.

Hearing brides discuss the nuances of Chantilly lace versus French brocade all day made her want to rip the rainbow-colored curls from her scalp. It was always the same gaggle of women, it seemed. Different faces and different names… yet always near-identical personalities when they opened their mouths.

The nervous-but-happy bride.

The subtly controlling mother.

The narcissistic Bridesmaids.

The distracted Maid of Honor.

She wasn't sure why she'd asked to get her old job back when she returned. Tonight, she just wanted to drown herself in hops and male attention the second she peeled out of the boutique's parking lot.

The bearded man beside her was now gawking expectantly, waiting for a response to an inquiry she'd been too disinterested in to hear.

"Hmmmm?" she hummed.

"I said, you have beautiful eyes. Are they real? Or are they fake? Like *contacts*?"

"Everything on me is real, honey," she said with a flirtatious wink and hopped off the bar stool. "Thanks for the drink. See you around."

"Hey. I'm a nice guy 'n all, so I'm not gonna be a dick, but, you know, *usually*, it's customary to at least *pretend* you're interested in the fella spendin' twelve dollars on a dollar-fifty beer," he grumbled, smile falling. "Just sayin'…"

She offered the long-neck to him. "Oh, sorry. My bad. You want it back?"

"Nevermind. Just… get lost." He waved her away, cursing under his breath at her sarcastic retort.

Chastity rolled her eyes and sauntered away.

This is why you are going to end up alone like some… harlot spinster, Chastity could almost hear her mother say. *Your abhorrent behavior brings shame to the Lord… and to* us…

According to her folks, 'God-fearing Christians' don't frequent seedy bars. They don't talk back to their parents or avoid church like the plague. And they *certainly* don't go back to random apartments with hot men who have deltoids made of solid rock…

Like *Barrett's.*

But wasn't Noah a *drunkard*?

And, hell, Paul *murdered* Christians.

Yet, according to the Bible and her father's Sunday sermons, those men were still allegedly aspirational. *So.. why was* she *somehow so unlovable?* Why had she fallen so far from their good graces by simply existing?

She supposed it was fate. Some women were destined for riches and fame, some for exciting careers, some for political and social endeavors, some for squeezing out a litter of children…

And then, there was Chastity…

An unstable contrarian with fried-and-dyed hair that seemed to do nothing but irritate the people in her life.

She took another long swig of her beer and silently wished she'd asked for something stronger to help her escape reality, even if just for a while. Still, the bottle of foamy hops soothed a little of her worry and washed away a tiny bit of the disappointment about herself that she'd clung to for the last few months.

Chastity graduating college was the untruth that her mother was pushing publicly, despite what the Bible says about lies, white or otherwise. Maggie was too embarrassed to utter the truth: *My daughter flunked out of veterinary school before graduation. She couldn't hack it. Not even for four more short, stupid months.*

The diagnosis changed Chastity's life, one that scared her, shook her confidence, and made her come crawling back to Jackson to live with her parents. Now, she felt like no one really knew her.

Including herself.

She scanned the room for attractive men, but her mind reeled with thoughts of the glossy pamphlet she'd been given, the one with the damning bold letters that read:

Living Well with Bipolar Disorder.

She recalled the overgeneralized suggestions within its folds almost as if they were memorized lines from a high school play. They were all things that seemed obvious but felt impossible.

Adopt a regular sleep schedule. Exhaustion can trigger mood episodes.

Chastity couldn't remember the last time she got a full night's sleep or went to bed at a regular time.

Maintain a regular exercise routine. Exercise releases endorphins, which can improve mood.

That part always made Chastity laugh. So does having sex. That's considered cardio, right?

Eat healthy and manage stress. Avoid triggers and practice relaxation with yoga and/or meditation.

How can one do that when life always bombards you with aggravating situations? That's life. Life is stressful.

Avoid drugs and alcohol. Substance use can worsen or exacerbate mood swings.

That was the one that bothered her the most, an impairment that would ostracize her at just about every wedding or social function. She was not addicted to alcohol. She could do without its awful taste and the hangovers. But drugs and alcohol sometimes took the edge off. They made her feel more… normal.

Enroll in regular therapy sessions. Find a counselor or therapist. A psychologist can evaluate your moods and habits and prescribe medication to lessen symptoms. Discuss coping techniques. Learn to identify triggers and mood swings.

She refused to let a hair-brained quack turn her into some emotionless zombie.

Sure, the lows were *low*. She *had* thought about ending it all. A few times, in fact. Church had taught her that suicide was an unforgivable sin, but damnation wasn't what kept her alive. It was something more, the waste of potential that it all would have been if she had taken the easy route. Somehow, inexplicably, she could always see through the fog enough to know that taking her own life wasn't the answer.

And the *highs* of being bipolar…

The highs were intoxicating. The thought of ever dulling that with medications so that she could be like everyone else made her want to scream.

For years, she had no idea that she'd even been experiencing manic and depressive episodes. Still, now she wondered if the *mania* was what was *keeping* her alive, keeping her tethered to this world, keeping her from making a choice she couldn't ever come back from on days like today when she felt swallowed by that familiar sense of dread.

The psychologist had been blunt and brief in his diagnosis. Her mind was a tsunami of whirling thoughts and pain followed by an overwhelming sense of loneliness for the weeks that followed. It was devastating to know that once people heard that word, they'd assume they knew just about everything they needed to know about her.

Bipolar.

Not *kind* or *nurturing*.

Not *great with animals*.

Not *bright and talented*.

People would, instead, think of her as some nuclear bomb, constantly on the brink of detonation.

Something isn't quite right with her.

Those were her mother's words, ones she'd overheard for the umpteenth time, ones that landed her in that leather therapist's chair finally.

Chastity had made the mistake of telling her mother about her diagnosis the same night. Her mother's brilliant suggestion was to *pray it away* like a demon to be exorcised, like being bipolar was some sacrilegious act that one could beg for deliverance from.

She tried to explain to her mother that this was something she never asked for. Something she never wanted. Something she didn't bring on with an action. Something *she didn't deserve.*

Chastity set her empty bottle on the bar and heard one of the regular bartenders holler, "Another?"

Chastity shook her head. "Gimme a shot of tequila, and then cash me out. This place is dead."

The shot was in front of her in a flash and inside of her even faster. As the man behind the bar ran her already-racked credit card, her amber eyes glanced around at the men in the bar.

Even though she didn't know if he even frequented *The Alibi*, part of her hoped to see Barrett, hoped for more mind-blowing sex to distract her.

But he wasn't there.

The man handed her card and receipt over. She debated taking a drive over to the honky-tonk where she'd met him, debated making up an excuse to take a walk by his apartment, but as she scribbled her name and pocketed the card, she felt deflated. Thinking of her diagnosis did that a lot lately.

She decided instead to head home, back to her parent's place. The newest episode of *Summer Love* would be on. She could drift to sleep to the sound of petty arguments and dream of a life where she was someone else.

9

Tossing the covers back, Barrett fisted his granite erection in his grasp, stroking it with a death grip. He had regularly punished his cock since his blissful night with the woman who called herself Aphrodite. Something about the thought of her body made his dick weep. He pictured rolling her pierced nipples raised into pebbled peaks between his fingers. He imagined his tongue diving into the wet bliss of her mouth. He could almost feel his cock grind against her skin, skin that was wet and aching for him.

After a few minutes of frustration, he growled, once again unable to climax, a feeling of relief that had eluded him since he had been inside her.

Barrett stomped out of bed, snatched a pair of gray sweatpants and a muscle tank from a pile on the floor, and sniffed them. He deemed the outfit 'clean enough' and dressed for the gym, desperate to burn off some steam.

Urinating with an erection was a particular skill Barrett had thankfully mastered already. After, he washed his hands, snatched up his truck keys, and bolted out the door, relieved that his dick was already down to what he liked to call *half-mast*.

After a brisk three-minute drive, he parked and jogged inside, looking up at the cluster of birds nesting in the bright red signage of his local gym, *Swole*.

Inside, the delightful combo of sweat and cleaning fluid wafted at him. He glanced around, seeing a few groggy regulars who looked perturbed about having to sweat this early on a Saturday.

In one corner, a scrawny man in a hoodie struggled at a weight bench. Nearby, an exhausted woman, presumably a mother -- if the spit-up stains on her shirt were any indication -- climbed a stair-stepper, half-asleep. An old man whose loose skin clung to surprising muscle mass pedaled a high-end stationary bike. His form and physique were something Barrett hoped for at such an advanced age.

Nearby, a busty redhead deadlifted a set of twenty-five-pound weights in front of a wall of mirrors. Her firm ass and toned thighs beckoned him. He made his way next to her, picking up a set of weights and starting in on his alternating bicep curls. Playing it cool, he ignored her for a bit, stealing glances in the mirror when she lowered her head in concentration. After several repetitions, she glanced up, puffing air as she contracted her muscles. Barrett cast a seductive smile at her in the mirror.

Like fish in a barrel.

Only her expression remained flat. She returned her gaze to the checkered floor, focusing on the task.

"Your form is perfect," he finally said, pretending to admire her biceps but staring, instead, straight at her breasts in the mirror, ones firmly mashed down by a peach sports bra.

She never raised her head to look at him.

"That's fair. If I was a beautiful woman like you, I wouldn't want to talk to me either."

She jerked an earbud out of her ear, previously obscured by her shoulder-length red hair. Tinny whispers of death metal blared from it. "*What*?"

"I was just saying—"

"I'm here to work out, not find a man," she said curtly.

"Same," he said quickly, trying to be funny.

She didn't laugh. "You're barkin' up the wrong tree. I like chicks."

He laughed. "Whaddaya know? Me too. Seems we have something in common already."

"Yeah, makes sense. My gaydar was going off." She snorted, focusing back on her weights.

He laughed and pumped the weights harder, shaking his head. "I meant, I like chicks, too."

She stared at him in the mirror for a moment and then cracked a smile. "I'm Charlotte."

"*Me too!*" he exclaimed.

She laughed, weights dangling at the ends of her relaxed arms.

"Just kidding. Barrett. I haven't seen you around before. You just join?"

"Visitor pass. My brother goes here. I'm just in town visiting the poor sap." She nodded to the far side of the gym where the waif of a man sat on the weight bench, bright white calves on display below a pair of basketball shorts. He lifted his chin, looking around to see if he was in anyone's way.

Barrett immediately recognized his crooked nose and dark, sunken eyes. It was Anthony.

And he looked like shit.

"Wait, hold up. Anthony's your brother?"

Charlotte nodded.

"So you're *Char*! Like, *the* Char."

"No one calls me Char and lives. Except *him*." She threw a nod in her brother's direction.

Barrett lowered his voice. "He still on the rocks with Linda?"

She set the weights back down on the rack. "She left him. Went down to—"

"El Paso. Yeah, he was saying that last week when I ran into him at the bar. Thought he might have worked things out by now."

"Pfft." She shook her head, tugging sweaty strands of red hair from her neck. "Nope. My brother's a stubborn dick. He doesn't do anything unless it's *his* idea."

She leaned against the weight rack and shook her head. "He's gonna lose her. He spent the whole week chasing slutty little bimbos around. Frankly, I don't blame Linda for leaving him. Hell, I'd have kicked his skinny ass to the curb a decade ago if I were her, but she stuck it out this far. Strong woman."

Barrett watched Anthony wipe a tear from his face with the long sleeve of his hoodie, red nose shining like Rudolph's beneath the gym lights.

"You should go say 'hi' to him. He could use a friend."

"Yeah, I will." Barrett nodded solemnly, lowered his weights, and wrapped his arms around his chest, staring at the sad little mess his friend had become in just a few days, shriveled to a shell of his former self.

"Hey," he looked back at Charlotte. "You want some breakfast? There's a great place down the block. If you guys are hungry, the food's on me."

10

The Persephone Diner was a small breakfast spot within walking distance from *Swole*. Early birds and groups of elderly patrons chattered, filling the small building with a low hum of conversation, only to be interrupted by the odd belly laugh and the clatter of cups being refilled. A waitress, a middle-aged woman with tired eyes, poured the last of her carafe into Barrett's cup. After an appreciative and flirtatious nod from him, she blushed and hurried away.

Anthony and his sister sat in a red leather booth across from him, waiting for someone to break the awkward silence.

"What's going on with you, man?" Barrett asked, staring at his friend.

After a pause, Charlotte nudged her brother. "You gonna tell him, or do you want me to?"

Anthony's gaze remained stuck on his own coffee cup. It was as if his weary eyes silently begged the black liquid to make footholds, allowing him a way out of the hole he had dug for himself.

"Fine," Charlotte said. "He's been pretending he's an eligible bachelor and trying to live a sort of Playboy lifestyle. Except, he has no charm, no game, and the seduction style of Helen Keller."

Barrett snorted, bringing his coffee cup to his face to hide his smile. "I take it you didn't take my advice and go crawling back?"

A tear ran down Anthony's cheek, and he quickly wiped it away with the sleeve of his tattered hoodie. "No. And I'm glad my crumbling marriage is so amusing to the both of you."

"Did you tell him what you did?" Charlotte asked Anthony, setting her cup back down on the table. Beneath her zip-up athletic wear, the peek of her full sports bra drew Barrett's eye, even though he knew he had as much of a chance with her as a fish would at successfully riding a bicycle. She snapped her fingers in front of Barrett's face and jerked up the zipper on her skin-tight jacket. "You're here to help, not stare at my tits."

"Oh, come on," Barrett teased, "You, of all people, have to appreciate the lure of the female form."

"True." She nodded, turning her face back to her brother. "Go on. Tell him."

Anthony finally lifted his head, his eyes making contact with Barrett's momentarily before flicking away again. "She served me with divorce papers, man. It's over."

Wide-eyed, Barrett stared at him. "What? What the hell happened?"

With a pressing glare from his sister, Anthony continued, "I… kissed someone. It was stupid."

Barrett laughed. "We talkin' *above* the belt or *below* the belt?"

"Would you knock it the fuck off?" Charlotte snapped, drawing the other quiet patron's attention.

"You're right. Sorry. This is serious. Okay, so you kissed someone… presumably other than your wife?"

Anthony nodded solemnly. "She was an old friend. It just sort of… happened. It wasn't that big of a deal. At least, I didn't think it was. It was a mistake. I was hammered. I never said anything to Linda because I knew it would just piss her off. It's not like I fucked the girl."

"Yeah, but you see why it's still shitty, right?" Charlotte asked.

"Of course." He grimaced. "Couple weeks later, word finally got back to Linda. And she freaked out because the people that told her said we did more, and I looked guiltier than I was because I'd hid it from her. It was just a kiss, she's blowing this shit way out of proportion."

Charlotte slapped Anthony's head and leaned back in the booth. "And that's why you're a fucking idiot. You don't accept responsibility. Hold yourself accountable. Be a man, Anthony."

"She's right," Barrett said.

Anthony shot him a glare and pushed up on the table. "Look, I'm dealing with enough. I don't need more shit from *you* two."

Jerking the fabric of his hoodie, Charlotte held Anthony in place. "Sit your scrawny ass down. We're not done."

Anthony pulled the fabric out of his sister's hand and sat, crossing his arms. "I kissed someone! Big-fuckin-woop. Linda's acting like I knocked the bitch up. It was one stupid kiss!"

"Where's Linda? You want me to talk to her?" Barrett asked.

"She's still down in El Paso! Said she's having a lawyer draw up papers as we speak."

"Maybe she's bluffing." Barrett shrugged.

"She's gone, Barrett. Won't answer my calls, my texts, nothing. I found out about the papers because she texted my *Mom*."

Barrett winced. It was worse than he thought. "What are you gonna do about the kids?"

"I don't fuckin' know."

"You seemed happy the other day, man. What happened to *Party Anthony*?"

"*Party Anthony* is who got me in deep shit, to begin with," he mumbled, picking at a chip in the table's laminate top.

Charlotte leaned toward Barrett, jerking her thumb toward her brother. "Now, instead of doing the legwork to smooth things over with Linda, he thinks he's suddenly got the license to be Hugh Hefner."

"What do you mean?" Barrett asked, trying to curb the grin plucking at the edge of his lips at the thought of Anthony in a satin robe with a babe on each arm.

Anthony straightened his posture, his voice angry. "Hey, if she wants to leave and take my kids all the way to fucking Texas, I figure I have every right to make the most of it."

"Oh no," Barrett mumbled.

"Yup!" Charlotte chimed in, slapping her brother so hard on the back his body jostled. "My brother's been fucking every willing wet hole in Jackson with a pulse." She laughed. "Moron already caught crabs."

"Oh, for fuck's sake," Anthony growled, collapsing into himself again. "You gonna tell everyone in town all my business? Jesus, Char, why don't we take out a fucking billboard?"

"They're pricey. You're lucky my girlfriend has expensive taste, or I'd have already nabbed one of those fuckers. Plastered your face right on the sumbitch," she teased.

Anthony shook his head. "We're *separated*. I'm allowed to do what I want!"

"Does *she* know you're separated?" Charlotte asked.

"Well, if she'd fucking *talk* to me, she would." Anthony looked at Barrett, seeking sympathy. "Come on. Of all people, *you* know how nice it is. Late nights. Beautiful women. Booze. Dancing. Loud music. *Freedom*. Real fucking freedom. Not sitting at home, listening to the old ball-and-chain bitch about her mother for the umpteenth time, or having her nag me for not helping around the house. No telling me to go jerk off because she has some kind of perpetual headache."

He leaned back and continued, "It's my time. If I wanna eat fried chicken for every meal, nobody is going to tell me not to. Watch porn in the living room? Who's gonna stop me? I married Linda straight outta high school. I never got to live your life, Barrett. See, you had it right all along. You're too smart for that shit. You never shackled yourself to a mortgage and marriage. You're out there just bein' free. Relationships are a fucking trap. You saw it, but

I couldn't. You always knew to cut that shit loose before it got too serious."

Barrett leaned forward. "So if this is *the life*, why do you look so fucking miserable?"

"I dunno." Anthony's lip quivered.

"I'll tell you why, Anthony. Because the grass *isn't* greener on this side of the fence, motherfucker. It's a paved *parking lot* over here. You wanna live like me? You wanna be a playboy? Fine. Cut your hair. Shave your damn face. Work on that doughy-ass body."

The waitress arrived with their plates. In front of Charlotte, she set down a bowl of oatmeal and fresh fruit and a plate of scrambled eggs in front of Barrett. She set a plate of French toast in front of Anthony, whose face temporarily lifted in a smile before falling back to its sullen stare.

"Thanks." Barrett nodded to the waitress before swapping his plate with Anthony.

Reaching for it back, Barrett blocked Anthony's hands.

"Those are yours now. Lean protein. It'll help you stop looking like a soft, pissed-off-looking little incel."

"What the fuck?!" Anthony groaned.

Barrett dug a fork into the sugary confection and lifted a bite of French toast to his mouth. His shoulders slunk at the orgasmic taste of dough and powdered sugar on his tongue. "You wanna pull quality ass, you gotta work on that body."

Glancing down, Anthony frowned. "Chicks like dad-bods!"

"You're a *deadbeat* dad at *best* right now. No kids, no dad-bod. Now, how much money you got?"

"Some. Not a lot. Why?"

"You've got a mortgage with one income, and now you'll have to pay for dates and a new wardrobe."

"My wardrobe is fine."

"No. You have work clothes and whatever this monstrosity is." Charlotte gestured to him. "Women don't want a guy dressed like the Unabomber, douche-bag. *You* gotta care before *they* care."

"You got away with that shit because you were married. Now you need date clothes. After this, we'll go shopping." Barrett pointed toward the door with his syrup-covered fork.

"I hate clothes shopping."

"I can tell," Charlotte said, jabbing her fork at his hoodie. "Tough shit. Linda's in the dust. Ain't nobody gonna dress you now."

Anthony stared at the French toast that was supposed to be his. "I know what you two are doing. You're just trying to scare me into going back."

"Not at all," Barrett lied, giving him his best smile. "I'm happy to have a wing-man again. It'll be great. Now, let's talk sex. What's your favorite position?"

"Oh God." Charlotte dropped her spoon in her bowl with a sharp *clink*.

"All of them." Anthony shrugged.

"Women like decisive men. Men in control. Men who know what they want. Now come on, favorite position?"

"Woman on top?" It was more of a question than an answer.

"Ugh. I'm gonna be sick," Charlotte joked, puffing out her cheeks like she was about to vomit. "I could have gone my whole life without knowing that."

"Well, saddle up, pardner, that's not your favorite anymore," Barrett said confidently.

"What? Why?"

"That's a lazy man's position. If you wanna blow a girl's mind, it's not gonna be from below. Sure, it's fun for you. But it's not memorable for her. It's not something that will make anyone come back for more. At that point, she could just get a suction-cup dildo and call it a day without all the headache and cleanup."

"They make those?" Anthony asked seriously.

Charlotte choked on a mouthful of coffee and quickly started snatching the napkins from the dispenser, covering her lips.

"Jesus Christ. You know what... let's work on your pick-up lines." Barrett scooted the plate away and leaned his chin on his knuckles. Batting his eyelashes, he widened his eyes and pretended to flip long, imaginary hair over his shoulder. "I'm a beautiful woman at a bar. Go ahead. Show me what you got."

Anthony's cheeks flushed red, and his eyes darted back and forth between Barrett and his sister. "Oh, come on. Char is right there."

"You don't think women are gonna have friends around? Or other guys trying to pick them up? You'll have to learn to do this with an audience, bud. Go ahead. Lay it on me. Show me the magic."

"Um... excuse me... Miss..."

Barrett loudly made the noise of a game show's incorrect answer buzzer.

"What was that?!"

"I said like four words!" Anthony groaned defensively.

"Anthony, that approach is great... if you wanna come at it like a caveman, bop her on the head, and drag the bitch home unconscious."

"Oh, like *you* could do any better."

Barrett turned to Charlotte and smiled. "Wow." He laughed and feigned a sudden expression of seduction worthy of an Oscar. "You're so beautiful that you made me forget my pick-up line. What do you say I buy you a drink while I try to remember it?" He reached across the table to wipe a droplet of coffee from Charlotte's lip. She recoiled at the contact, but he stayed in character. "Sorry, Sweetheart, you had a little something there."

Charlotte cackled and turned away. "And that's when I swoop and nab the woman right after you scare her off."

Anthony gritted his teeth. "I'm not incompetent. I managed to get Linda to marry me. I'm not fucking stupid."

"Alright, Casanova." Barrett's smile dissipated. "Let's say you've moved up to seduction master status. What then? Are you good with your life just existing around that? This week, you've seen all there is to see on this side. Dirty sex. Crabs. Drinking. Hangovers. Star-fishing across your bed. Sleeping with your dick out. Eating whatever the hell you want. Next week you'll start to realize that nobody gives a *shit* about you. Every chore in your lonely-ass day, it's all on you. There's no one to share the load of life with."

Barrett was getting flustered now, losing some of his cool facade as he continued. "See, you got duped by some cardboard 2-D version of what you *thought* life would be like without Linda. Tell me, what was so fucking awful about a woman showing you she cared about you every single day? About kids who needed you around to teach them about life, to teach them what to expect out of a real man?"

Charlotte shook her head. "Life is hard. People die. Shit happens to our bodies. We get laid off, lose our friends, and get swallowed up in a pile of bills. Stop and think about if you want to go through all the hard shit in life alone. Because Linda is there, ready to share those future burdens with someone. How fun will it be to see her sharing her life with someone else one day? Because lemme tell ya, she *will* move on."

Anthony pulled back his sleeve to look at a colorful beaded bracelet his son crafted for him with his favorite colors. "Even if I went to El Paso and groveled, there's nothing I can say that won't make things worse."

Charlotte pulled his face toward hers. "That's not true, bro. Start with 'I'm sorry. I'm an idiot. I made a huge mistake, and I want to make it up to you.'"

"That would mean you'd have to genuinely give a shit, though," Barrett said seriously, finally sliding the French toast to its rightful owner. "If you go, don't phone it in. You broke her trust. Earning it back is a process. If you're in, *be* all-in."

Taking a forkful of doughy deliciousness, Anthony felt the heavenly treat practically dissolve on his tongue. He snickered a little. "I could never look like you anyway. I love carbs and post-sex ice cream too much."

"Ewww! Again, I didn't need to know that!" Charlotte grimaced, shooting her brother another look of disgust.

Barrett laughed and set down his fork, suddenly losing his appetite. His smile fell. The talk had backfired. For the first time in a while, Barrett wondered if, in fact, *he* was the one who had made the wrong choice by spending most of his adult life playing the field.

Chastity wandered through the double doors of the animal shelter. The familiar barks and meows greeted her as she approached the front desk. Behind the counter, the reception chair was empty. Rodney had probably gone out for his morning *Starbucks* run.

Chastity signed in on the clipboard, tossed it back onto the countertop, and headed into the back room, looking both ways down the long perpendicular corridors. She turned toward the path to the canine kennels, the cacophony of barks drowning out any intrusive thoughts in her head. She shouldered a lumpy tote bag sporting the image of a duck with stuffed feet dangling from the bottom seam, kicking her softly in the thigh with every step.

She walked past each wire-front kennel, petting dogs through the metal. She reached into her bag and handed a small biscuit to each. She greeted them by the name on their white info cards before halting in the middle of the last row. She stood still, staring at the beautiful animal inside, a Mastiff. Its large, walnut-colored eyes stared back at her distrustfully from the far corner of the enclosure.

The other dogs hopped against their chain-link doors, but something about this quiet, brindle beast called out to her.

The Mastiff's door was marked with a red slip of paper with the dog's information. She read it carefully.

Name: Molly

Breed: Mastiff mix

Sex: Spayed female

Age: approx. three

Good with children: no

Good with dogs: no, but does well with cats.

Notes: Shy on first meeting. Recent surgery. Do not pet. Use caution. *Aggressive.*

She kneeled next to the cage and held her hand at the chain link so the animal could scent her. Molly sniffed the air and turned away, squeezing tighter into her corner.

"You frightened, girl? You don't have to be. I'm... a *lot* of things, but scary isn't one of them," Chastity cooed.

Molly didn't move.

Chastity looked around, scanning to see if the coast was still clear of Rodney or any of the others. Before she'd left for college, when she had volunteered previously, she'd been warned repeatedly not to enter the cages of the animals marked as aggressive. It was dangerous and reckless, a liability for the shelter. But, stubbornly, Chastity often did it anyway.

At one point, Rodney had even threatened to have her removed from the volunteer list permanently, but in such a small town with such a minuscule budget, the place was too desperate for unpaid help to effectively ban anyone who wanted to share the workload.

Lifting the latch, Chastity stepped inside Molly's kennel, closing the gate behind her. The Mastiff watched, cowering, ears raised at the sight of her small space being invaded.

Chastity slunk down to the floor near the door, ignoring the overpowering stench of urine and bleach in the air. She grabbed another biscuit from her bag and offered it, but Molly turned away.

Chastity slowly set it on the floor between them, watching the dog flinch as she leaned closer. Molly's lip twitched as though she might bare her teeth but decided against it.

"I'm gonna leave that for you. For later. I'm Chastity. It's nice to meet you, Molly. Although full disclosure, there's not really an animal I've met and didn't like." She glanced at the untouched treat and then back at the Mastiff.

"You seem to have a bad reputation." She smirked. "Me, too."

The dog's eyes finally met hers.

"Bite-risk, huh? Did you have a bad day? It happens. Or was it the volunteer? You know, some of these people are just here for court-ordered community service," she said bitterly. "Not me. I'm here because I want to be around you guys. It makes me happy."

She pointed at the paper zip-tied to the other side of the gate. "That thing doesn't tell me what makes *you* happy. Or what your favorite toy is. Or if you're secretly a cuddle bug. Your existence has been boiled down to a few words. Now everyone thinks they know you and that they can *judge* you on those words. Hell, I can relate."

Molly eyed the treat again and thought better of it. Instead, she walked in a half-circle, looking for a place to lie down. It was only then that Chastity saw that the huge animal only had three legs, each attached to a snow-white paw. Finally, the dog collapsed into a furry mound on an old, rectangular dog bed and sighed.

Chastity relaxed, looking at the clear amputation scar a few inches below one of Molly's hip bones, reddened stitches irritated. Molly turned her head, flapped her jowls with a few lazy chomps, and rested her chin on her front paws, warm eyes still staring.

"We scary ladies are the ones who need love the most, aren't we, girl?"

The dog let out a snort as if to somehow agree.

Chastity smiled and pulled a book slowly from her bag. "Mind if I read to you?"

Silence.

"Great. I hope you are a fan of paranormal romance. If you're not, just give me a sign, okay?"

Molly just stared at her from the dog bed, occasionally eyeing the treat between them.

"This one's about two orcs who hate each other, but they've been forced together, and now they're starting to realize they might actually *like* each other."

Chastity read a few pages aloud. Sometime during the next chapter, Molly crept on her belly and snapped up the treat. Chastity smiled, still reading, seeing the dog drool in her periphery. She placed another treat in the same spot and continued on.

Moments later, Molly scooted closer, timidly gobbling it up, too.

By the end of the second chapter, Molly had shuffled close on her belly, close enough to reach out and pet. Chastity flipped the page and set her hand on the floor, giving Molly the chance to smell her. By the end of the next page, Molly gently licked her hand.

"I'm fresh out of bones. All I can offer is pets."

Chastity hesitantly placed her palm on Molly's head and rubbed between her ears. The Mastiff let out a low groan of pleasure and puffed air out of her jowls. Then, she slowly set down her book and stroked Molly's face and neck tenderly with both hands, savoring the trust that she'd built with a little patience.

Molly had what people saw as a defect. She sat by herself, day in and day out, feeling unloved and unwanted. Chastity felt her eyes well with tears at the parallel in their lives. She wanted to rip the red piece of paper on her cage to shreds. Every other dog in the place would soon find a forever home, but gems like Molly would most likely continue to be overlooked.

From behind her, Chastity heard a pair of tennis shoes squeak to a stop. She knew the footfalls well, the limp of the gait. She smiled as she caught sight of him through the fencing.

"Girl, I *know* you know you're not supposed to be in there," the man said playfully.

Chastity smiled. "Well, look what the cat dragged in."

Rodney was a brittle old man who loved animals even more than she did. Despite having arthritic hands and knees, he never hesitated to kneel on the floor and give love to any and every creature who wanted it. Semi-retired now, he was a man who devoted decades of his time, and even some of his pension, to keep the shelter afloat.

"You just can't stay away from the naughty ones, can you?" His green eyes still shined bright with youth despite the wrinkled eyelids around them.

"I was always taught in Daddy's church, *'You have to go where you are called.'*"

Rodney opened the door to the kennel beside her, riling all the other dogs with the squeak of the hinges. He wrapped a lead around the neck of a rowdy rottweiler. Chastity could smell its breath from feet away.

"I know, I know. I'm happy to see you, too," Rodney said, watching the dog spin donuts at light speed. "I see we have some extra energy today. Let's go out to the yard and play while Miss Erikson here corrupts Molly there with her dirty smut books."

Chastity smiled. "You know me too well."

"Oh, it wasn't a guess. I heard ya. Came around the corner and heard something about an orc performing fellatio, and I felt like I had to make my presence known." He snickered. "You know I have these virgin ears and all."

Chastity blushed. *Maybe it wasn't the most appropriate material to be reading aloud in public…*

Rodney took the excitable dog outside, and the other pups quieted down. Chastity read her book in silence, calmly running her fingernails along Molly's scalp until the dog was snoring as loud as a human.

12

The home's facade was made up of varying shades of slate-colored stone that stood out against the afternoon's dark clouds. After a flash of light, Barrett heard the faint rumble of thunder and pursed his lips. He was grateful he was going inside, where the rare spring rain could pour down to its heart's content. It seemed like it never rained in Wyoming anymore.

We need the moisture, he could hear Gam-Gam say in his head, something she uttered every time there was precipitation without fail.

He carefully pulled onto the grass near the mailbox. The driveway was full and carefully edged despite the dead, yellow grass in the yard. It would be at least another week or two before it was warm enough to sprout anew.

His dirty Jeep felt inadequate compared to the other seven high-end sedans parked bumper-to-bumper on the concrete drive leading to the house.

The property looked expensive, especially with its nearly unimpeded view of the Grand Tetons in the distance. Neat junipers sat next to columns flanking a black front door. To either side were floor-to-ceiling patterned windows that blended seamlessly into one another. The building was positioned on an expansive plot of land featuring acre-upon-acre of natural perfection. The place was nicer than he'd imagined for a pious pastor. He'd expected something... more modest. Even humble, perhaps.

Barrett killed his truck and rushed straight across the grass to the door, eager to get inside before the sky opened up and soaked his formal attire. He pressed the doorbell and rocked on his heels, hands tapping a cheap pen against a legal pad.

Moments later, Maggie tugged the door open. Her hair was curled into waves, and light makeup accentuated her classic features. She wore a silk blouse tucked into tweed trousers, punctuated by a pair of sensible Mary Janes.

"I'm sorry," Barrett pointed to the double rows of cars to his right, "Are you hosting right now? I could have sworn Stella said we were meeting this morning."

"Oh shoot, I forgot that was *today*," she said, pounding the heel of her hand against her forehead. "Well, come on in..."

She looked at him, trying to recall his name.

"Barrett. Barrett Andrews," he offered.

"That's right. I do apologize. Our flock has grown, and I have gotten the regulars down pat, but I still struggle with some of the more *sporadic* attendees."

He followed her in, whacking the pad against his slacks nervously.

"Come. I'll introduce you to all the ladies." Maggie chuckled, leading him down a long hall toward a towering archway that led into a spacious room.

As they neared the end of the hall, a stained-glass door to his right swung open wide.

As soon as he saw the face beyond, he was floored, frozen in place. At first, he thought his mind was playing tricks by showing him the breathtaking face he'd been daydreaming about all week. But the longer he stood, trying to bat away the hallucination with rapidly fluttering eyes, the more he realized…

She was really there.

In the flesh.

That oh-so-smooth flesh burned into his mind.

She emerged from the bathroom in a plume of steam and jasmine perfume, body wrapped in a cotton bathrobe, slit open between her thighs almost enough to catch a glimpse of Heaven's entrance.

She was stunned, too, still like an animal facing a predator with no way out. Her vibrant, rainbow ringlets dripped onto the tile. Her eyes never blinked.

"Hi."

The second she uttered the single syllable, Barrett's heart began to pound.

He assumed that she, like so many others, had simply been passing through town, a tourist on her way to see Yellowstone, a vacationer passing through toward Devils Tower.

But she *lived here.*

She lived in *Jackson.*

The thought of her being within arms reach made Barrett feel lightheaded.

"Uh… hi."

Okay, so he wasn't Shakespeare.

"It's good to see you, Barrett."

"Pleasure's all mine, *Aphrodite.*" He smiled wide and bit his lip sensually while eyeing her up and down. "I tried to call you, but it was the darnedest thing. Kept ringing through to a Chinese restaurant."

"Best Asian buffet in Northwestern Wyoming." Chastity smiled smugly. "The crab rangoons'll change your life."

Maggie groaned. "Um, excuse me, young lady, we have *guests!*"

"*So?*"

"So?!" Maggie's voice was high and annoyed. "So, why are you washing up on this side of the house? What is wrong with *your* shower?"

"I like *this* tub." Chastity's eyes flashed to Barrett's. "The Jacuzzi has some *really* powerful jets that you can *aim* if you know what I'm sayin'." She flashed him a filthy smile and winked. All of the blood in his upper half drained to his cock in an instant. All traces of the English language evaporated momentarily from his brain.

"I don't know what you're getting at, and I am sure we do not *want* to know." Maggie shooed her daughter down the hall. "Go! Now! Get dressed! Stop walking around half-naked like a hussy."

"Mary Magdalene was a hussy, and she—"

"Go!" Maggie interrupted, angrier now.

Chastity started down the hall with a satisfied smile, waltzing backward so she could keep her eyes locked on Barrett.

Maggie turned at the end of the hall and walked off, muttering, "Kids. I swear she is trying to turn me prematurely *gray*."

Just before Chastity was out of sight, she opened her towel, flashing Barrett the entire front of her tattooed body, naked and dripping.

She was freshly shaven and even more perfect than he remembered.

At that moment, Barrett thought he might faint.

Chastity disappeared into a room, and Barrett finally found the nerve to move again, covering his crotch with the notepad. He followed Maggie's direction and turned into a living room full of older women in earth tones, all somewhere between forty-five and *ancient*, seated on couches and dining chairs in a casual circle. Susan Glenecky was among them.

"Susan," he said with a cordial wave.

"Glad you could make it," Susan said joyfully.

"Please, Barrett, have a seat," Maggie said, setting a dining room chair next to one of the women for him.

Confused, he nodded politely and sat.

"Now ladies, I hope I'm not here to judge a *Miss Wyoming* contest because, in my book, you'd all be winners," he said in an attempt to charm them. Being so close to his grandmother for years, he knew how to get along swimmingly with women in their age bracket.

Lie out your ass, lay on the charm, and don't ever fuckin' cuss. That, in Barrett's mind, was the key to success with anyone with varicose veins.

Several women giggled and nudged one another before falling quiet again.

Barrett cleared his throat and chuckled. "I think I must have gotten my dates mixed up. I came over to clean. I feel like I'm interrupting something."

"Not at all!" crooned the woman beside him. She patted him on the thigh with a delicate age-spotted hand.

Another held up a gold-plated book. "We just finished up Bible study, and we were gabbing about our family troubles. We'd talk all day and night if you'd let us." She started to reach for her purse when Barrett spoke, addressing the group.

"You know," he tapped his pen nervously, thinking about their gathering as an opportunity, "You ladies seem like you know a thing or two. Maybe while I've got you all here, I could ask you all a couple of questions."

"Well... sure! Ask away," Susan said, volunteering their help.

Barrett looked around at the women. "Well, you see, I just got this new gig cleaning houses, and I thought I'd be really good at it. Like it'd be *instinctual* to know how to clean and all. But," he laughed, "turns out I don't know nearly as much as I thought I did. I never really learned how to do this stuff. My parents died when I was nine. My grandmother, Stella, she took me in—"

"Oh, Stella! I *adore* Stella," another woman said.

"She's a doll-baby," Susan chirped loudly.

"I'm sure she'd be glad to hear that." Barrett smiled. "See, when she took my brother and me on, she really had her hands full. I guess we were too busy makin' messes to ever learn how to clean 'em up."

The ladies giggled.

"Stella's a good woman," Maggie said. "I imagine most boys don't get taught those things, especially if there's a woman around to cook and clean *for* them. My mother had me making dinners for the whole family by the age of twelve."

"I can't even imagine," Barrett said reverently. "I'd just really appreciate any tips or tricks you fine ladies could give me. I really would like to keep this job. I'm already on thin ice. I nearly got fired on my first day for exploding a lady's rug in her fancy dryer and melting a hole through some towels that were about the same price as the down payment on my Jeep out there."

The woman on his other side piped up. "I'd be happy to teach you what I know. I owned a dry-cleaning business with my husband, God rest his soul, for twenty-some-odd years." She patted his thigh, and her expression changed as she cackled. "Oh my, feels like you're made of *marble*!"

The woman blushed and laughed as she removed her hand. Barrett could see traces of Pepto-pink lipstick on her dentures. "Are you single, Barrett?"

"Yes, ma'am." He nodded.

"Maggie, this is the one I was tryin' to get you to introduce to Chastity," Susan said. "They would make such a lovely pair, don't you agree? She should be so lucky to end up with a strapping young buck like Stella's boy."

Maggie scoffed. "They just met. She waltzed out in a *towel* a moment ago. No couth, that one."

"She's a wild one," Susan cackled.

Maggie added, "Barrett seems like far too nice a person to do something like that to. Handsome boy like him could have any woman he wants."

It wrenched Barrett's soul to hear Aphrodite's mother talking about her like that. He was a bargain-bin Chippendale's dancer with a bleach bucket in Nowhere, Wyoming.

He didn't deserve a woman like *her*.

Then, her name settled in his mind. *Chastity*, Maggie had called her. He wanted to laugh at the irony.

"I just love that she had the guts to do that rainbow thing to her hair," one woman said.

"*Ombre*."

"Is that what it's called? Ombre?"

"That's what my beautician said."

The women all started chatting quietly, Chastity's vibrant rainbow curls at the center of every topical conversation at that moment.

Barrett cleared his throat, and the ladies all seemed to quiet down at once.

"I couldn't pull off a rainbow ombre," the woman next to Barrett said, cutting through the silence. "I'm stuck with this boring ol' gray."

"Proverbs chapter sixteen, verse thirty-one: '*Gray hair is a crown of glory*,'" a new woman's voice said from the entrance to the kitchen.

The voice was familiar, but not Aphrodite's. Older...

Barrett's head turned toward it, narrowing his eyes as he spotted Sue Thompson coming from the kitchen with a tiny paper plate full of deviled eggs in her hand. His stomach flipped at the sight of her. He wanted to run, wanted to bolt straight through the wall at the sight of the woman who nearly just got him shit-canned. But he didn't move, didn't budge.

Sue's tight smile met his. "Couldn't help but overhear you needed some cleaning tips." She laughed, a kind of laugh that advertised it was a private joke. "*Lieutenant.*"

After a strange moment of silence, one of the ladies in the living room spoke. "Let's start with laundry. How do you do your own laundry? What do you do?"

Sue laughed so hard she nearly choked on a boiled egg white.

Barrett's eyes never left hers, suddenly feeling the intense scrutiny. "I, uh, take it to a laundromat, put the clothes in a washer with some detergent, set it to hot, and push start."

Sue cackled and stuffed the rest of the egg in her mouth. "Explains a *lot.*"

"Do you separate the lights and darks?"

"Do you know what settings to use?"

"Are you using liquid or powder detergent?"

The questions were firing rapidly from the women.

"No," Barrett said, "I didn't know you needed to separate them. I just use normal settings, I guess. And sometimes liquid, sometimes powder. Depends on what's cheapest at the dollar store."

"Oh boy," the woman next to Barrett said with a sigh, stealing another feel of his thigh, "We have a *lot* to teach you."

***

Later, in the kitchen's breakfast nook, Maggie and Barrett sat drinking hot tea. The house was quieter now that the Bible study group had gone home. Barrett scribbled notes down on his pad. Maggie kept tapping at the yellow paper with her French tips.

"… And another thing. Grout can be tricky. I used to clean bathrooms at a local hotel. That was always something people commented on, how *nice* the bathrooms always were. I left them spotless." She smiled with more pride than Barrett thought the comment warranted.

"Take pride in the small things, and God will do the rest."

Barrett nodded. "What kind of cleaning supplies do you recommend for that? Are there brands you like?"

"Oh yes. I'd be happy to make you a list of everything to use. I'll have it next time you come. But don't wear your Sunday best. You'll be on your knees scrubbing, and what you're wearing now is very… *inappropriate.*"

Oh, God… if she only knew.

Maggie smiled and patted Barrett's hand. "It'll be nice to have some help for once."

"The pastor isn't the cleaning type, I take it?"

Maggie chuckled. "No, not at all."

Barrett smiled, then swallowed, trying to broach a subject that had been nagging at him for two hours. "What about your daughter? *Chastity*, is it?"

"Pfft. She's here in body only. Her mind is somewhere far away since she came back." Her face grew sullen. "We don't have the best relationship."

"Oh," Barrett said, realizing he had taken a step onto shaky territory.

"She's an only child, and she's got the ego and selfishness that goes with it. She's stubborn as a mule. Gets that from her father. If she doesn't want to do something, ten men and an act of God couldn't get her to do it."

She looked out the window, staring at the retreating clouds as she continued. "There were complications with her delivery when she was born. I knew then she'd be my only child, and because of that, I suppose I coddled her too much. And now she's sort of... adrift. She's twenty-five and acts like she's *twelve*."

Maggie rolled her eyes and watched as a whitetail deer skittered over to her bird feeder.

"When I was her age. I had a husband *and* a house. Arnold and I were already starting our church, small as it was back then." She laughed. "His first service was out of a dilapidated mobile home in the poor part of Moran if you can believe it."

Barrett smiled. "Sure, I can."

"Arnold and I were focused on making a real difference. But she, of course, didn't follow suit. She is a brilliant girl, but something isn't… *quite right* with her. It's quite embarrassing, really. Between you, me, and this table, she's only back home because she flunked out of college."

"Oh."

"Her last semester, mind you. Instead of dusting herself off and trying that last one over again, she just up and quit completely. Walked away. All that veterinary training for nothing. Just… a real waste, if you ask me, of money, time, and dreams. And now she's back here acting like she can just come and go like I run a free motel."

"Must be tough to watch someone squander that kind of potential," Barrett said softly, trying to soothe her.

She nodded. "We've spent our entire adult lives helping to shepherd a flock, and now our only daughter is the one wayward sheep we can't seem to keep with the herd."

Just then, Barrett saw someone in his periphery, someone leaning against the kitchen's entrance with a scowl.

It was her. His infatuating rainbow-haired beauty. Aphrodite.

No… Chastity.

"*Speak of the Devil*," Maggie said, slapping her palms to the table.

Barrett spun and smiled at her, tapping his notepad like a drummer. "Well, hello. *Chastity*, was it?"

He tried to hide his smile, tried to hide the fact that he already knew her *intimately* in front of her mother.

Chastity crossed her arms over her tank top, one sporting a cute cartoon mushroom holding a bloodied butcher's knife. Her jeans were snug and low, showing a delicious sliver of her abdomen that he longed to run his tongue along again.

Chastity looked past him. "Maggie, where did you put my purse? I need it."

"Why do you *insist* on calling me Maggie? It's so disrespectful. Does '*Honor thy Father and thy Mother*' mean absolutely nothing to you?"

"She's a *quick* one," Chastity muttered sarcastically to Barrett.

A smirk settled on Barrett's lips.

"Where are you going?" Maggie inquired.

"Oh, well, I was thinking of breaking into the church with a bottle of wine and a roast pig and hosting an orgy on the stage. You know, just a little good old-fashioned debauchery. Maybe even do like a Sodom and Gomorrah theme and put out a charcuterie board in case people get extra hungry from all the fellatio."

"Stop! Just... stop!" Maggie opened her mouth and closed it several times before finally saying, "I put your purse in the coat closet."

"Thanks," Chastity bit out before turning back to Barrett. "Nice to meet you, Barrett."

"See you around?" he asked, hopeful.

"Maybe." She shrugged and walked down the hall.

"You alright, Mrs. Erikson?" Barrett asked quietly.

"The *filth* that comes out of that girl's mouth sometimes!"

Barrett thought back to their night together in his apartment...

And of the filth she was willing to put *in*.

It made him hard just thinking about it.

"Right. Anyway, *windows*. *Windex* is kind of the standard as far as cleaners go. If you use paper towels, you're often going to end up with streaks. There's an old trick I use where you rub the glass with a piece of *newspaper,* and it'll be so clean that birds'll end up trying to fly right through it."

Barrett knew whatever vulnerability he had seen from Maggie was long gone. Her face had changed back into the well-practiced expression of a cheery pastor's wife, the only part of herself that she probably ever allowed the world to see.

13

This client's home was unlike the ones Barrett had been told about. Located in a gated community, the simple two-story house was nestled in the middle of a row of homes, all nearly identical. Cotton-white siding made its brown shutters and newly-budding hedges pop.

He double-checked the address on his phone.

Yup. This had to be it.

It wasn't what he expected after Sue Thompson's sprawling manor. By no means was it any mansion. This... seemed like a family home.

Barrett slung a black duffel bag on his shoulder, grabbed a pail of supplies out of the back of his Jeep, and strutted to the house. He started up the steps and nervously tripped up the last one, slamming down shoulder-first onto the wood in front of the door.

"*Ow, fuck,*" he whispered, collecting the fallen fluids and scrub pads before rising to his feet. He whispered to himself, embarrassed, "*Not off to a good start, are ya, Dip-shit?*"

He knocked hard and rubbed his shoulder, watching a chain-suspended bench swing sway in the cool breeze as he waited for someone to answer.

A short, Hispanic woman with wide eyes opened the door. "You must be from *Man Maid*."

"Yes. I'm Barrett, your Norse God. Are you Ms. Aguilar?"

"Yes. Just… you can… call me Maya." She seemed flustered, smitten by his appearance, even in his street clothes. She shut the door behind him with rosy cheeks and a bashful smile.

"Great, Maya, do you suppose there might be somewhere I can change into my, uh, uniform?"

"Oh, of course. Right this way." Maya led him to a small bathroom to his right.

Barrett stripped, quietly managed twenty push-ups and thirty crunches and re-dressed quickly, bursting forth from the cramped room in a movie-quality Viking costume.

"*I am Odin*," Barrett growled at the top of his lungs, "*God of war and death!* I will not stop until your home sparkles like the floors of Valhalla!"

Maya laughed, covering her face. She was turned on and embarrassed in equal measure as her eyes took in the details of his attire.

Brown fur pads rested atop his bare shoulders attached to a cloak, the straps of which crisscrossed across his oiled, muscular chest in a leather 'X.' His pulsing forearms bulged out of matching leather bracers with intricate silver scrolled designs.

Just below the muscular dip of his abdomen sat a pair of shiny brown leather shorts that fit his rock-hard ass like tight briefs. The fur of his calf-high boots was grazed by the bottom of the cloak, the ensemble pulled together by his sex appeal and sudden confidence.

Maya's syrupy brown eyes darted back and forth over his muscles, tanned cheeks blooming a bright hue of red.

"My dearest Freya," he said, scooping her into his arms. She yelped like a woman at a male revue and buried her face in his neck. "Show me, my dearest, what room you would like me to get started in."

"Um, the kitchen."

He groaned theatrically, voice booming through her living room. "Lead the way, darling Freya!"

***

The modern kitchen was lit brightly with swirled-glass pendant lights. Beyond it, chocolate-colored cabinets with copper details gave the room a strangely welcoming feel. The cocoa-colored walls in Maya's uncluttered home were devoid of personal photos, showcasing only framed, impersonal wildlife photography in its stead.

As he scrubbed the backsplash behind the copper sink, Barrett took notice of its contents. One bowl. One plate. One coffee mug and a single empty wine glass. She lived alone, and she clearly didn't socialize often.

He cleaned them all carefully, applying the tips Maggie and the other devout women had given him, careful not to shatter her delicate stemware.

Behind him, Maya stood in the doorway, watching him work. She was wearing his cape around her neck. He put it on her once it became cumbersome, as it had been blocking her *view* anyway.

He turned to her and smiled, shaking his wet hands over the sink. "Maya? Are you alright?"

"Yes, of course. I'm sorry, was I being awkward? I do that sometimes. I don't get a lot of company."

"Are you and Mr. Aguilar homebodies?" He knew the answer already.

Her smile fell a little. "There is no Mr. Aguilar."

"What about a *Mrs*. Aguilar?"

She chuckled. "No wife either. Kinda just… married to my work, I guess."

"What do you do?"

"I'm a software developer."

"Cool. Like, video games and stuff?" he asked, moving down the counter. He lifted up a cookie jar and started wiping it down with a damp cloth.

"No, nothing fun like that. Mostly boring stuff. Well, at least, to others."

"Workin' on anything right now?"

"I'm troubleshooting one we just built, actually. I developed a program for a few laboratories that intelligently analyzes and accurately integrates peaks in gas chromatography. Then, it creates a report for the customer. Between the tweaking and patching, trying to get things fixed before launch, I haven't had much of a social life."

"Holy shit, so… you're really intelligent."

Her face beamed with pride despite her shy smile. *This was a woman who lived to work.*

"I don't know about all *that*…" She tucked a strand of black hair behind her ear.

"Sounds like you're a heck of a lot smarter'n me."

She stole a glance at his shiny ass before averting her eyes.

He stared at her out of the corner of his eye and mischievously grinned. "You don't have to sneak-a-peek. You paid for this show. Gawk freely."

"Feels... weird." She laughed. "Feels rude to stare."

"Odin is here to give Freya a show." He set the cookie jar down, wiped more of the counter, and then started hosing the microwave down with antibacterial spray.

There was a long pause before Maya spoke again, weak and unsure. "Can I ask a weird question?"

"I have nothing but time. Fire away, Freya."

"Am I... attractive?"

The question caught him off-guard. Barrett turned to face her, furry boots clacking on the tile floor, afternoon sun glinting off shorts so tight she could almost see his religion. He held the microwave's turntable in his hands, wiping it with a rag. "Excuse me?"

"I mean... just... like, objectively, from a male point of view? I'm... I'm not trying to come onto you. I just figured... with you here...

dressed like that... I figured we were past formalities, and I could just ask you honestly."

"I think you're beautiful," he said genuinely. Then he laughed. "But, I don't know how much weight that holds. If you ask around, people will tell you I find a lot of women attractive."

"A bit of a womanizer, huh?"

"Womanizer sounds mean and, like, calculated. I prefer to think of myself more as a dabbler, of sorts."

"A *player.*"

"A *lover.*"

"A real Romeo."

"Hey," he laughed, "don't you slut shame me! Just because I'm a Norse God doesn't mean I don't have feelings."

"Sorry that I asked. I know that was... inappropriate."

"If you weren't a client, trust me, I'd have hit on you by now."

"You're just saying that."

"No. Men should be tripping over themselves for you. Although, you're probably living a lot more stress-free life than some of these *married* chicks."

"True." She nodded.

"I like my life the way it is most of the time. I like my solitude. I just get lonely, too, sometimes."

"You should go out. Go dancin'. That's what I do. I love a good Cotton-eye Joe."

"I'm not the line-dancing type."

"What kinda *type* are you, then? You like to cha-cha? Waltz?"

"Try pole." She laughed and covered her face.

"Excuse me?"

"Hold on. Oh my God, I can't believe I'm showing you this…" Maya disappeared into the living room, rifled through a few things, and came back with an eight-by-ten portfolio.

Barrett placed the glass plate back in the microwave and folded his arms across his baby-oiled pecs.

Maya flipped the page open to one of the plastic-sheathed photographs inside and shoved the book toward the Viking God in her kitchen with a look of embarrassment.

"Holy shit! Is that you?" Barrett asked, snatching the portfolio fully away from her. In the book were blurry snapshots of a woman dancing on a chrome stripper pole at what looked like a dance club. In one of the images, the woman was upside down, holding the rod, doing splits in the air.

"Jesus, Mary, and Joseph!" He flipped through the pages to another where he saw a photo of a younger Maya holding a first-place award.

"I didn't even know they had competitions for this kind of stuff. Dammit, I want to be a judge!"

"I was a wild child. First place in the New Mexico pole dancing competition... three years in a row," she boasted. "Although, you'd never know it now that I've packed on about twenty pounds."

"Oh, stop it. You look amazing." Barrett flipped through more pages, each an incredible shot of an animal. The book was full of prints of peacocks, jellyfish, monkeys, and crustaceans.

"Did you take all these?"

She nodded and waved it away. "Yeah, but you don't have to look through those."

"These are incredible."

"I used to photograph for a bunch of magazines. That was before I learned C++."

He closed the book and looked at her with sincerity. "You're a cool chick, Maya."

She smiled, too embarrassed to respond. She took the book and plopped it on the kitchen island, backing up to her original vantage point in the doorway.

"What's that?" She pointed to the corner of the floor. "On the grout?"

Barrett looked around, confused. "Where?"

"Right there. On the grout in the corner on the floor." She smiled. "Looks *real* dirty right there."

What she was insinuating finally occurred to Barrett. "Oh, that? On the floor?"

He pointed to nothing.

"That? Oh wow, what a mess. That's going to need a good scrubbing. Do you mind if I get down on my knees and get it soaking wet so I can *really* go to town on that thing?"

He lowered to his knees, grinning the whole way, sticking his shiny ass in her direction, muscles flexed.

She laughed, cheeks blushing again. "By all means. Don't mind me. I really do adore when you're... *thorough*."

14

"You nailed it. I don't know what you said or did this time, but Ms. Aguilar was thrilled," Will said through the phone.

Barrett balled his free hand and pounded it into the air, whispering, "*Fuck yeah!*"

"She said to tell you next time, 'Freya wants Loki.' I'm ordering a Loki knockoff costume right now."

"You need my sizes again?"

"Nah, Ava keeps 'em all in a book. She's so fuckin' organized it makes my head spin sometimes."

"Oh man, I'm so relieved she liked me. Am I off probation now?"

Will laughed. "We'll see. I'm just glad it went well. She's over the moon. Think you might have just gotten yourself your first regular. I'll have outfits all ready for tomorrow, so just swing by the shop at seven and pick up the go-bags."

"Ugh, seven?"

"Yeah, that means you'll probably have to hit *Swole* at six. They're open then, right?"

"Yeah, they're a twenty-four-hour gym."

"Good. In the morning, you've got an eight-thirty as Elvis Presley in *Three Creek Ranch*, and in the afternoon at two, you're out in *Shooting Star* dressed as… a naval sailor."

"Elvis? Like young Elvis, or, like, obese-toilet-Elvis?"

"Which one do you think, genius? Let's use our brains."

"Geez, wow. My boss is a dick."

Will laughed hard on the other end.

"These costumes are lame. Why don't these women ever pick any of the cool ones?"

"Barrett, I promise," Will sighed, "you will get to wear the Jack Sparrow soon. I'll… run a discount on that one or something. Five percent off the fee if they choose it."

"Fuck, man, if Ava wasn't marrying you, I'd step up to the plate *myself* and wed your ass."

"We wouldn't mesh well, Barrett."

"Why?"

"Because I'm, like, a nine… and you're a three."

"Oh fuck off, I am not a three. Ask Aguilar! I am a *God*!"

"God of toe fungus."

"Hey, Fuck-stick, I just had a pedicure recently."

"You're such a girl."

"Speaking of, who do I turn in the receipt to? I can expense that, right? It's a write-off."

"Yeah, right. Ava's gonna check with the tax accountant and see if your fuckin' *spa days* are reimbursable," Will teased.

"I'm picking up sarcasm, Mr. Jessup. Keep it up, and I'll leave you. I'll call our wedding off."

"I wouldn't marry you if you *paid* me, Barrett."

Barrett groaned into the air and looked around his apartment. It looked like a bomb had gone off. "That pedi was fifty bucks!"

"*You're* a pedi!" Will giggled. " Pedi-*file*."

"I don't know how you can *possibly* joke about these things. Y'know… after your uncle touched you in your *no-no spot*—"

"I don't *have* an uncle!" Will laughed hard. "Fuck off, Barrett. Go to bed."

Barrett tried to fight his smile. "Alright. Love you, brother."

"See you tomorrow, Dingleberry."

"Yeah." Barrett ended the call and threw his phone onto the couch. His smile disappeared. Something about knowing his partner in crime was settling down with a wife and a family made him feel slightly nauseous.

146

Will was yet another casualty of suburban war, doomed to a life of cookie-cutter houses, H.O.A.s, man-caves, 'perfect lawn-height' discussions, and imported beers.

Commitment wasn't what scared him. It was the unromantic contractual agreement where people gambled away half their assets that freaked Barrett out. His urge to keep the same woman around for a while was nonexistent, and the permanence of putting a ring on someone's finger had simply never appealed to him.

He wondered if he would ever find himself in a relationship, one where he could be all-in. No rings. No engagements. Just loyalty and a ravenous desire to be with one another. He wanted one day to love *hard*, to love *fierce*. And when that woman was his, he'd be protective as hell.

Meowwwwwww.

The sound was muffled by the window, snapping him out of his moody thoughts. A charcoal British Shorthair cat sat, perched on the roof near the abutment, minty green eyes wide and helpless.

"Heyyyyy. How's it goin', Smoky?" Barrett asked happily. "I missed you, girl!"

Jogging over, he flicked open the latch on the dormer window and pushed it open. The cat sauntered in like she owned the place, long tail flicking from side to side.

Barrett closed the window behind her. "You're just in time for dinner. You and I will be dining on these," he shuffled over to the paper bag on his kitchen counter, "*exquisite* cans of dolphin-safe tuna. You'll love it."

He briefly held the tips of his fingers to his lips and pulled them away in a chef's kiss.

Piercing the first can, he heard Smoky let out a pitiful *meow*.

"You know what to do." He pointed to the tiny dining room table. "The place may be a shithole, but we are still civilized beings who eat at the table, you and I."

Smoky wandered to the table and leaped up on it gracefully. Moments later, Barrett dropped an opened can in front of the cat, and the animal lapped at it greedily, scarfing down the meat like she hadn't eaten in days. Barrett sat in the opposite chair and ate out of his own can with a fork.

Despite Smoky -- a name he'd given her because she looked like she'd just survived a house fire -- being feral, he'd still worried about her safety during the five-day absence.

Once she'd finished, Smoky leaped off the oak, whipping several unopened bills and month-old junk mail off the side. Something metallic *tinked* on the floor.

Barrett reached over to pick up the strewn mail and saw Chastity's earring there on the wood. He picked it up and shook it, heart wiggling freely inside the rib cage and making him smile.

He remembered how she'd flashed him fresh out of the shower right around the corner from ten ultra-conservative strangers.

She was a wild one.

He wanted more than anything to be with her again. Tasting her. Feeling her. *Holding* her.

He plunked down on the couch and shook the earring again, like some sad prince with only his soulmate's glass slipper as a memento.

But unlike that prince, Barrett had already found his Cinderella. She was living at home with her preacher father and frustrated mother.

Not here…

In his bed. In his *arms*.

He rolled his eyes, irritated with himself for the sudden hopelessly romantic thoughts. Still, the urge to see her again plucked at his gut.

He wasn't certain where he'd gone wrong, what he'd done to warrant a phony number, what he'd said to make her so aloof at Maggie's when he said he wanted to see her again.

That night that he'd brought her to his home, the look in her eyes was intense, filled with desire, with *want*.

So… what had changed?

Where did he go wrong?

Were there red flags that scared her off? Another woman's balled-up panties among the piles, perhaps? Aside from a filthy apartment, he couldn't see any other items that warranted such a cold brush-off.

Smoky climbed up into Barrett's lap and curled into a ball. He stroked her head softly, and within a minute or two, she was purring. He thought it best to put his thoughts of Aphrodite… of *Chastity*… aside for the night.

After all, looking down at Smoky, tired from her adventures out in the world, he could appreciate that some things were best left wild and untamed.

15

The muffled cackling of old crones made Chastity's eyes flit open. She stretched and mumbled, "This place is like a geriatric denture convention."

She threw her legs over the side of the bed, snatched her phone from the nightstand, and did a double-take.

Three p.m.

Are you fucking kidding me?

She wondered how that could possibly be accurate.

She fell asleep bingeing the prior season of *Summer Love*, a cleverly edited elimination-style reality TV show filmed every summer where half-naked hotties hooked up in will-they-won't-they show-mances followed by a whirlwind of drama and sex.

She thought she might have dozed off somewhere around midnight, just before Tawny, a double-D-silicone-breasted bitch, was finally voted out of the beach house. But… if that was the case, *why had she slept in so late?*

After weeks of piss-poor sleep, that had to be… what? *Fifteen hours* of snoozing? Surely, that couldn't be right.

Bible study was in full swing in the living area just a little beyond her door. Every word felt like sandpaper in her ear, grating on her sanity, grinding her paper-thin patience to a pulp.

Chastity trudged to the dresser and snatched out a clean black bra and green panties, quickly changing into them before throwing on a tight pair of leggings and a cherry-red, low-cut V-neck that said, '*Don't be a prick*' with a small waving cactus printed on the right breast. She scrounged two socks at random and sat to put them on.

One woman's words trickled in through the gap beneath her door. "So… she got *kicked out* of the university?"

"No! Didn't you listen? She *flunked* out," another old biddy said.

"Why? Why wouldn't she just take the semester over?" asked yet another voice, one belonging to a woman old enough to have signed Jesus's birth certificate herself.

"Well, I guess it's not that much of a stretch. I heard the poor girl was *already* on academic probation."

Another gasped. "Oh my! For *what*?"

"My sister-in-law's daughter is on the board down there. She said that Chastity was caught with a half-naked boy in the women's dormitory—"

"No!"

"—And they were smoking *reefer*."

Chastity almost snorted at the outdated term. She threw on her boots and grabbed the doorknob, hesitating to open it.

"That's a shame. She had so much potential." She heard the woman make a *tisk* sound.

"Weed is a gateway drug," another voice chimed in.

"I can't believe she's on *the pot*. Such a shame. You know, I knew she'd seemed off since she's been home."

"It *would* explain some things."

"I should say this quickly before Maggie comes back, but she told me that something is *really* wrong with the girl. She's been seeing a therapist. He put her on medications and *everything*."

"Oh, my."

Chastity stepped back from the door.

Her mother told them?

When her mother couldn't *pray* the bipolar away... she, what? *Told* people about it?

That wasn't her business to tell!

153

Chastity listened to these women drone on about her. As if any of them had ever really known her at all. A void opened inside of her, swallowing up all sense, her anger building into a righteous rage.

"It's always the good parents that get tasked with the most difficult-to-love children. God gives his greatest battles to his strongest warriors," said that *damned* first voice again.

"I was just reading this book about a girl who was possessed by a demon. I wonder if Chastity has been playing around with a Ouija board."

Chastity's eyes welled with tears threatening to overflow.

"Lucifer was an angel, too, once. Such a shame. I'll be keeping Maggie and Pastor Erikson in my prayers."

"Me, too."

"What are we talking about ladies?" Chastity recognized the voice as her mother's.

"Oh, just last Sunday's sermon," one said quickly.

"Well, I brought some cheese cubes and crackers out in case anyone was hungry."

Chastity threw open the door and stomped into the living room. She fought to control her anger.

"Afternoon, ladies. Having a productive Bible study, I see."

"Chastity! It's lovely to see you!" One woman said, swallowing nervously, wondering how much she'd overheard of their conversation. "I didn't realize you were home! I thought for sure you'd be at work... or the shelter. Your mother's told us you do volunteer work over there sometimes."

Chastity's eyes were wild, tone carefully clipped. "I don't have a Ouija board."

The women all looked horrified.

She'd heard everything.

"I'm also not possessed, I do smoke pot occasionally to take the edge off, and the boy in my dorm was *fully* naked, not half-naked."

One woman gasped and clutched at the collar of her dress.

"Be-cause we had been fuck-ing." She emphasized the words. "And after we finished the joint, we were going to go for round three."

"Chastity!" Maggie yelped. "What is going on?!"

"Ask them! Ask your *posse* of chatty little hens, all clucking about my issues like they give two shits about me!" She looked around the group of women. "Not *one* of y'all know me, so keep my damn *name* out of your mouths, you gossiping... old... *hogs*."

The women stared back at her blankly, unsure what to say.

"Well, I never!"

"Yeah, you probably have never done a lotta things, you old codger."

"Chastity, stop! You cannot just barge into my Bible study and *berate* our flock while you live under my roof!"

"Ohhhhh, *fuck your flock*!"

A second woman gasped this time.

"You want Bible study? Why not look at some passages that are applicable to you, huh?"

Chastity waltzed up to one of the women and snatched the Bible off her lap. She flipped through pages wildly until she found the first passage. "Let's see, James chapter one, verse twenty-six says, '*If you claim to be religious but don't control your tongue, you are fooling yourself, and your religion is worthless.*'"

Her eyes flitted to one of the women. "I saw your son's name in the paper a while back. Got arrested for possession. Had a... *what did the paper call it?* Oh yeah, a dealer's amount of crystal methamphetamine in his car down at the *Loaf 'n Jug* right there by the junior high. But, hey, according to *this*, I should probably mind my own business on *that* one, shouldn't I?"

The woman didn't even blink. The others watched Chastity's furious flurry of page-flipping.

"Ephesians chapter four, verse twenty-nine says, '*Do not let any unwholesome talk come out of your mouths, but only what is helpful for building others up according to their needs, that it may benefit those who listen.*'"

"Enough!" her mother screamed. But Maggie's plea fell on deaf ears.

"No, no, I got another one. Psalm chapter one-hundred-and-nine, verse three. This one you're gonna wanna highlight, flock. '*They encircle me with words of hate and attack me without cause.*' Hmmm... Ladies? Sound familiar?"

"I said that is enough!" Maggie rose from her seat, though her shout never phased her wayward daughter.

"Guess that theology class you insisted I take is biting you in the ass now, ain't it, Mother?"

"Chastity, I swear..." Maggie was at a loss for words, fuming.

Chastity closed the Bible loudly and pointed to one of the ladies. "Where is your husband, Anne? I'll tell you. He's shacked up with a girl half his age that he met two months ago at *The Alibi*. And, Mary-Jo, everyone knows you pilfered proceeds from last year's church carnival to buy that Kors purse because Herald cut you off."

Maggie stomped her foot. "Chastity Marie Erikson, I want you out of this house!"

"Suit yourself." Chastity shrugged as if her plans had not just been knocked into a complete tailspin. "Well, ladies, that should give you plenty more to jabber about. You're *welcome*."

Chastity started out of the room, stopped, and turned. "I'll get my things when you're at Sunday service. Don't worry. From now on, you won't have to see your *disgrace of a daughter* anymore. Maybe consider adopting some needy African orphan or something so you can mold them into the wholesome version of whatever it is you expected *me* to be."

Chastity turned so hard that her rainbow hair swung. She stuffed a few items into an overnight bag and hurried out to her car, leaving the stunned group of God-fearing women in silence.

16

Chastity sat outside of *The Rabbit Run Apartment Complex*. She'd withdrawn every last measly dollar in her account and every bit of cash advance she could get from her credit cards, setting aside her last hundred bucks for enough gas and food to get her through until her next paycheck, hoping it would be enough. She shakily handed a check over to a landlord whose skin looked like a worn leather bag. The woman sat, bleary-eyed and chain-smoking, in the dingy front office as Chastity signed the six-month lease agreement for the complex's only available unit.

She had snatched it off the market, sight unseen. After having been shot down by every other apartment complex on her list due to having zero rental references or the landlords not having any units available, Chastity knew her only other options were a greasy motel or the back seat of her car if she wanted a place to sleep.

Rabbit Run required no background check or references, a thought that simultaneously overjoyed and worried Chastity. The decrepit landlord had even done her a solid and knocked six hundred bucks off the move-in amount because of the alleged state of the apartment. There was an understanding between them before she would be allowed to sign that Chastity would be on her own to clean it if she wanted to move in right away, as the last tenant had been forcibly removed only a few days prior.

She agreed without hesitation. Surely, a little elbow grease would make the place sparkle like new in a jiffy, and it might even endear her more to the unit. Plus, with no real friends that she could couch-surf with, Chastity needed a place -- and she needed it fast -- as springtime in Jackson Hole was no time to be sleeping in a sedan with a janky heater.

As the woman took the check, Chastity suddenly felt settled. The two-and-a-half thousand bucks she'd just forked over for first, last, and security was a small price to pay to be out of her parent's house.

It was the monetary price of freedom.

Sure, things would be Ramen-noodle-tight for a long time, but college had taught her how to survive on a fast food Value Menu. With the reduced calorie intake, she would be swimsuit-ready by summertime, too, which was her glass-half-full way to look at it all.

For now, a Goodwill sleeping bag on the floor would be her bed, and the clothes in her trunk's "Ho-bag" -- an emergency supply bag she kept for use after one-night stands -- would have to suffice as a pillow. In her mind, anything was a marked improvement from where she'd just left.

Up a dank stairwell and along a hallway lined with faded faux wood panel walls and ugly halogen bulbs, she found it.

Apartment 208. Four hundred square feet of apartment, every inch of which was hers.

She slid the key into the lock and pushed the door open. With a satisfied smile, she flicked on the lights. The expression vanished immediately, melting into a sorrowful frown.

She looked around, watching her breath fog in the air as she took in the horrific sight. The apartment was freezing and, yet, smelled like a frat house. Beer bottles and empty cans lay scattered on the ground. Warped solo cups sat atop a full sink of disgusting dishes. Old pizza boxes sat on cluttered piles of junk. Dirty underwear and drug paraphernalia were piled all around the linoleum, leaving only a grimy path through the place.

Taking a few steps in, she saw what she hoped was only a clump of hair in a corner beside a smattering of empty mini liquor bottles.

On the wall, in Sharpie, were curse words, one-liners, scribbled pentagrams, and various other doodles she couldn't decipher.

The blinds on the bathroom window sat askew, gnarled into something that resembled a piece of abstract art. A blow-up doll sat half-inflated in the bathtub, the word 'PIG' written on it in lipstick. The walls were covered in what looked like shaving cream. Something viscous and gelatinous, like petroleum jelly, was smeared onto the small mirror above the sink. The toilet no longer had a lid, and a doll with no hair and one arm poked out of what was likely a bowl of someone's pungent, dehydrated urine.

In the next room, leaf litter was strewn onto the damp bedroom carpet from an open window, presumably left that way to air out the stench of cigarettes and stale vomit. There were stains of various colors that would require several carpet cleanings.

She was afraid she might have a panic attack at the state of the place. She leaned against a wall and lowered herself to her butt on the scummy floor, breathing rapidly, all too aware that she'd just sunk all the money she had into the shitty little dump before her.

Panic gripped her chest, and she struggled to breathe. She thought back to what she had read about the *four-eight-four* breathing technique and forced herself to focus.

Four seconds to breathe in.

Hold your breath for eight seconds.

Four seconds to breathe it out.

During her breathing, her phone buzzed, and an opportunity to mentally escape presented itself. She looked at the name.

Marcy H.

Her coworker at the bridal boutique. An acquaintance at best.

Why would she be calling? Had she missed a shift? Chastity was *certain* this was her day off.

Then, her stomach dropped. She hoped Marcy was not calling to tell her that they were letting her go, not after she'd just signed away almost every damn dollar she had.

"Hello?" Chastity sounded timid, fearful that this was not going to be good news.

"Hey, girl!" Marcy sounded jovial, possibly even drunk. At work, the girl hardly ever cracked a smile.

"Marcy? Is… everything alright?"

Marcy giggled for a long time. "Of course! I'm at this… house party. My boyfriend's friend's *friend* invited us. You should see this place. It's freakin' enormous!" She giggled again. "That's actually why I'm calling. You should come down! Have some fun! Everyone's on 'E,' and the vibe is sooooo good. We got a keg, too."

Chastity wanted to say 'No.' The thought of socializing with a coworker in a setting with booze and ecstasy felt like a recipe for disaster.

Her eyes drifted around the former trap house she'd found herself renting, and she suddenly felt a desperate need to escape.

"Sounds fun. Can you text me the address?"

"Hell, yeah! I'll send it right now." She giggled harder, even though nothing was funny. "Bring a bikini if you want. A bunch of us are playing a make-out game in this old lady's big ass hot tub!"

17

"Randall Bryant Nussbaum, what the hell is this?!" Sherri Nussbaum screamed, motioning to two stripped-down kids in their early twenties making out on her pool table. Beside her, others stood, some in bras or shirtless, covered in stripes of neon body paint, each carrying red plastic cups with a look of horror on their faces. Two more were on the spiral staircase, unwilling to halt their heavy petting long enough to pay her any mind.

"Shut… this party… down!" Sherri howled, her tight, perfect ponytail of salt-and-pepper hair swinging like a pendulum as she whipped her head around. "Everyone… go home! I swear to God, I will call the police! Is that what you want?"

"For what? They're all over twenty-one, Mom. Just *chill*," Randall muttered casually before taking a swig straight out of a bottle of Hennessy.

"Chill? You want me to be fucking *chill?* You didn't work for a goddamned thing in this house. I did!" She poked herself in the bony chest so hard it left a red mark.

Her stormy gray eyes glanced around. "Get out of my house! All of you! Out!"

She stomped the heel of her Manolo Blahnik's on the marble floor so hard that it snapped off, nearly toppling her over. She caught herself on a Roman pillar, nearly taking it and the thirty-five-thousand-dollar Ming vase atop it to the ground.

As some of the strangers reluctantly filtered out the front door, Sherri scrambled through her purse and found her phone. She dialed, tapping a long, beige nail against her pursed lip.

Finally, the person on the other end picked up.

"Yes, hi, Mr. Jessup. I need your services."

A young, shirtless man smiled at her, and she shooed him away angrily.

"I'm afraid it can't wait. Tomorrow, my husband is coming back from a work trip to Canada to celebrate his birthday, and tonight, my idiot son decided to throw a fucking *rager*."

18

Barrett's truck rumbled into the driveway. Sherri Nussbaum's long legs carried her briskly toward him as he killed the engine and grabbed a bag containing the same pleather Roman gladiator costume he'd cleaned a home in just a few hours before.

"Oh, thank God, you're here." Sherri placed an icy hand on his forearm and pulled him toward her home, cleavage bouncing above her oval neckline.

"I assume you're Mrs. Nussbaum?"

The woman nodded. At the door, she released him. "Start wherever you want and do me a favor. Don't wear any silly costumes right now. My dip-shit son is in there somewhere, and I don't need him using it as some weird form of blackmail against me down the line."

"I'm relieved to hear you say that. I wore it this afternoon. It hasn't been laundered yet."

"Well, at least *one* of us is relieved." She rolled her eyes.

"With all due respect, why call for me, then?"

"Excuse me? I don't follow." She crossed her bony arms across her silicone bosom.

"I just meant, *Man Maid* charges more than most *because* of the costumes? Why not just hire a regular cleaning service and save the money?"

She stepped toward him threateningly despite her calmer tone. "Will Jessup has been cleaning this house for a year-and-a-half now, and he does a damn fine job, a lot better than any service we've hired before. We used to hire some Mexicans to do it. Caught one of them robbing our DVD shelves blind, helping herself to a couple of movies every time. When we fired them, they went to the Tribune and made up a nasty bit of news about my husband."

"I see," Barrett rubbed his bottom lip.

"Will has a business founded on *discretion*. It's a huge part of the whole schtick. So, I called him, and he sent you."

"Don't worry. I'll have this place spic-and-span right away, Mrs. Nussbaum."

"I know you will. I'll throw in a cash tip if you keep the volume down. I got a splitting headache from screaming at those damned kids."

She started to walk past the pool table, looked down at a stain on the felt, and winced. She turned back to Barrett. "If you see any stragglers, tell them not to let that front door hit 'em where the good Lord split 'em on their way out."

"Sure thing."

"*God*, my head is *pounding*," Sherri muttered again.

"Here," he said, digging in his bag and pulling two pills from a small container. "Will keeps an emergency stash of ibuprofen in the bags for our aches and pains. Being on your knees a lot can be painful."

She took the pills and motioned all around, scoffing. "I know. How do you think I ended up with all of this?"

He tossed the pills in her mouth and winked. Barrett was relieved to see she actually had a sense of humor, after all.

She threw her head back violently and attempted to dry-swallow. She winced hard and fanned herself, frantically looking around for a drink to help the pills go down. Panicked, she looked at one of the solo cups on the edge of her billiard table, sniffed it, and took a swig out of the mysterious liquid with reluctance.

"Oh God, I hate when that happens! Ugh." She looked down at the stranger's cup and feigned gagging. Then, she turned back to Barrett.

"There's a box of trash bags on the bottom of the stairs for all this garbage. Mops are in the kitchen pantry. Sponges are under the sink. I'll be in my studio if you need anything, although I doubt yoga is going to undo all of this." She motioned to her head and disappeared through an archway.

Barrett stood for a moment, struggling to take it all in. The Nussbaum's massive mansion screamed decadence behind all of the fraternity-esque trash.

Artwork covered the walls, pieces that Barrett was certain he could have finger-painted himself. A winding staircase with a gigantic chandelier above it swirled up to a second floor with maroon walls and bronze fixtures. Hanging from a golden wall sconce was a woman's lace bra. The black walnut floor was littered with various spilled liquids and empty cups. Beer and liquor bottles sat on nearly every flat surface. Cigar butts littered ashtrays, filling the area with the stench of ash and tobacco.

He returned to his Jeep, tossing his bag inside and trading it for his pail of cleaning supplies.

Once in the house, he decided to start upstairs and work his way back down, assessing the extent of the mess as he toured the mammoth building. There, the bathrooms were in disarray, but the majority of the guest rooms were still in order. He turned down the bed in one room, fluffing and chopping the throw pillows and doing a quick pass for stray trash.

The next one was easier still as the bed was still made.

As he approached the third room, he heard the rustle of covers. He rolled his shoulders back, eager to assert dominance right off the bat to get the errant party people inside to kick rocks. He burst in through the door, and a lump beneath the silken comforter writhed, squirming at the noise of the intrusion.

"Hey, you. You don't have to go home, but you can't stay here. Out," his voice boomed.

"Barrett?" a muffled female voice called from beneath the covers.

The mention of his name made him curiously quirk an eyebrow. "Yessss, blanket goblin. And you are?"

The comforter pulled back, and the instant her mess of rainbow-colored hair came into sight, he froze.

Chastity's cheeks rose, her left sporting a smudge of neon green paint, and on the right, there was a smear of deep purple. The look on her face was one of embarrassment, with a smile that said, '*What are the odds?*'

Her shoulders were bare, and the way she clutched the blanket to her chest and the presence of a torn condom wrapper on the floor by a large pair of men's running shoes told him that she was naked beneath the sheets.

Part of him was thrilled by her sudden presence, especially in a state of undress. Seeing her always felt like being on the crest of a roller coaster and watching the death-defying drop below shoot toward his face.

"Fancy meeting *you* here." He smiled a little. "Three times in one week. That's gotta be some kind of a sign."

His excitement dissipated the moment a man darted past Barrett into the room, a kid in his twenties with no muscle mass and large globs of green and purple on his own cheeks.

"'Scuse me." He scrambled to pick his shoes up off the floor and held them up as if to say '*Found them*' before slipping past Barrett again and barreling down the staircase.

The sight of the kid, the condom, and Chastity's bare shoulders wrenched Barrett's gut with jealousy.

"I'll leave you to get dressed," he said, closing the door.

"Wait. Barrett, please don't make me go home." She looked like she was going to cry. "It's fucking disgusting there."

"Chastity, I've been to your home. It's nicer than any I've ever lived in."

"No," she groaned into the air and threw her head back on the pillow. "I moved out. I got a new place. Literally, today. It's... I can't even talk about it."

Barrett thought for a moment, still annoyed by the boy's intrusion and the thought of his Aphrodite being sullied by some loser who didn't even have the balls to kiss her beautiful lips goodbye before he bolted. He thought about how, if she were *his*, she would never leave the house without knowing how wild she made him.

"Please," she begged, the sound of the word like music to his ears.

"Tell you what," he sighed and spoke quietly as if Sherry Nussbaum was eavesdropping. "I'm tired. I've been on my knees scrubbing ladies' houses all day. If you wanna get dressed and help me tidy this place up, you can crash at my place."

His eyes focused on the condom on the floor. "My couch is weirdly comfy."

"I know." Chastity smiled a little.

"Hope you like cats because Smoky's crashing at my place right now, too."

"Smoky?" she asked, but Barrett had already started down the hall.

***

Shoving another fire-engine-red cup into a trash bag, Barrett snickered.

"What?" Chastity asked, wobbling on the tiptoes of her untied, checkered Vans, trying to reach a discarded bottle of Jack Daniels lying on its side atop a fanciful grandfather clock. When she couldn't quite reach it, she looked around and spotted an ottoman, dragging it over to the ornate timepiece and climbing on it.

As she reached again, Barrett's eyes skimmed up from her once-again mismatched socks to her trim legs, settling on the smooth, creamy thighs displayed beneath the hem of her short, tight, spandex dress. He bit his lower lip and shook his head at the perfect, round curvature of her ass.

"You could've just asked me to grab it for you instead of struggling like that. You're stubborn."

"Always have been." She finally managed to get the bottle down. "And *clever*. See?" She shook the remnants in the bottom comically before tossing it to him.

He caught it, barely, fumbling it twice before finally gaining possession. He frowned and tossed it into the black sack in his hands.

She climbed down and kicked the ottoman back into place, dusting the fabric where her shoes had been. "Not all of us are six-four giants like you."

"What are you? Four-eleven?"

She made a face at him and set her fists on her hips. "Ha-ha. You gonna make a *Hobbit* joke next?"

He chuckled. "Wouldn't dream of it."

"I'm five-five. That's still a *respectable* height. You're acting like I'm some kind of munchkin. I'm actually the perfect height to scrunch down and box someone in the balls for making fun of me," she threatened.

"Why are you little people so aggressive? Geez. Don't take it out on me just because you're vertically challenged. I'm devastatingly handsome, and you don't hear *me* complaining about it. Cougars *love* me. I can't go to any gathering of women over forty where I'm not getting numbers shoved at me, so, hey, we all have our crosses to bear."

She laughed. "Oh, you fucking poor, gorgeous sap. That must be just *awful*."

"You kiss your mother with that sassy-ass mouth?"

His retort changed the mood of the room in an instant. Chastity's playful banter halted at the mere reference to Maggie.

"She and I are not on speaking terms right now. I moved out, and I'm pretty sure neither of my parents give two shits."

"Sorry to hear that. Wanna talk about it?"

"With you?" She snorted. "No."

Barrett reeled back, furrowing his eyebrows. "Why not? I'm not just a pretty face. I can be a good listener, too. Lay it on me. What'd you do, say 'shit' at the dinner table?"

She placed a shredded throw pillow in his bag, packing it down. Barrett tied it closed, their faces only feet from each other, heat radiating through the air between them.

Tossing the bag to the side, Barrett grabbed the next empty from the roll and draped it over the arm of Nussbaum's antique tufted camelback sofa.

Chastity kneeled, pressing her face to the carpet to look beneath the couch. She spotted an empty beer can and reached for it.

Barrett watched as her firm ass hoisted high into the air, wishing she was at his apartment, stark naked, in the same readied position so that he could be inside of her again, watching her mop of colorful hair bounce forward with every pounding thrust of his hips from behind. He struggled to keep his cock from stiffening.

She spoke, shaking him from his fantasy. "When people know you're the pastor's kid, you're supposed to act like a *saint* day and night. You're under this, like, constant scrutiny. It leaves no room to be human. You're bound to be a disappointment no matter what."

She sat back on her heels and tossed the dented can into his bag.

"You're anything but a letdown, Aphrodite."

She smiled at the mention of the fake name. Barrett held out a hand, and she rose to her feet without his help.

"See? Stubborn."

She pointed at the trash bag in his clutches. "You maids get paid well to do this?"

"Maybe *most* don't, but usually, I'd be doing this in tiny Flash Gordon underwear. The hourly rate is a little better than my last job hauling heavy-ass furniture all around, but if you do well, my buddy says the tips are sometimes incredible. It's true, too. Had a chick tip me like two hundred bucks yesterday for a four-hour gig."

"Holy shit."

"Yeah, and all I did was clean her office and scrub fly shit off her chandelier."

"That's it?"

"That's it. I mean, of course, the tip was surely because of my sparkling wit and stellar conversation."

"Of course." She laughed. "Wasn't the washboard abs at *all*."

He smirked, popping a few Lysol wipes out of a barrel-shaped plastic container on the glass coffee table and wiping neon body paint off of the upright piano. He tossed the sheet in his bag and grabbed a fresh one.

"Come here for a second." He waved her over.

She stepped toward him, unable to take her eyes off of his.

"Hold still." He dabbed softly at her cheeks, wiping away the face paint smeared on them, a visual reminder that she'd recently been face-to-face kissing someone else.

Her amber eyes glinted from the light of a wall sconce with someone's tank top looped around it. "Oh my God, did my mother *hire* you to come clean our house in your underwear? Was that why you were at my house?"

Barrett laughed and released her, her cheeks now paint-free.

"No! Oh, God, no. My grandmother's friend, Susan, volunteered me at church to come over and clean. She heard I was a maid but didn't know... you know, the *rest*. But, I had just botched my first gig... hard... so your mom kinda took me under her wing. She and the ladies from the Bible study ended up giving me all kinds of tips and shit."

"Huh." Chastity felt slightly dazed by her mother's confusing display of kindness.

"I think we're good in here. Let's hit the hallway next and then go attack the foyer and that billiard area. I think that's all we have left."

She nodded and followed behind with the full bag and the barrel of wipes. Barrett grabbed any trash along the way, chuckling to himself about how this felt the way court-ordered highway cleanup looked in the movies for people in trouble with the law.

"Do you sleep with any of your clients? Do some of them pay extra for that?"

"No. *Apparently*, that's a huge no-no."

"Yeah, I mean, technically, I think that counts as prostitution, right?"

"So they say." Barrett turned to her. "They're usually not my type, though, and I *do* have a bit of a type."

"Oh yeah? What type is that?"

"Short, feisty, stubborn trouble-makers with dyed hair." He winked and turned back around. "Oh, and nothing gets me harder than a pair of mismatched socks."

"You should talk to a therapist about that," she joked. "Sounds like you have *terrible* taste."

"Well," he said, turning again and whispering in her ear. "You could always kiss me and learn *all about* my taste *firsthand*."

His words sent ripples of gooseflesh down her body, metal-studded nipples stiffening through the spandex.

"Been there. Done that." Her teeth dug into the side of her pouty bottom lip, and she made a checkmark in the air with her finger.

Just then, Sherri Nussbaum stumbled into the foyer, grinning from ear to ear, landing on the spiral staircase with a dull *thud*.

Barrett approached. "Mrs. Nussbaum, are you alright?"

Sherri laughed, seemingly delighted by the fall. Barrett looked around, confused. Sherri's broken heels were off, and there had seemingly been nothing on the floor to trip her.

"Who are *you*?" Sherri laughed, eyeing Chastity up and down.

Embarrassed, Chastity panicked, opening her mouth to speak and closing it again.

"She was a straggler. She offered to help. Figured you'd want us out of your hair as fast as possible, so I put her to work."

Barrett pulled the woman back onto her feet, and Sherri erupted into full-blown honks of laughter.

"What's so funny?" he asked, alarmed by her complete change in demeanor from his arrival. "Have you... been drinking, Mrs. Nussbaum?"

"Sssssssherri! Please. For God's ssssake," she cackled, ready to piss her pants with laughter, "Call me Sherri. And no…" She laughed so hard she wheezed. "I haven't… had anything."

Her laughter grew so intense she was no longer even making any noise beyond a quiet hiss. Her face grew red.

Chastity pulled Barrett to the side a few feet. "She's high," she said confidently.

"On what?" Barrett felt out of his element, unsure what to do.

"Fuck, if I had to wager a guess, I'd say ketamine or weed. Even LSD, maybe."

"Ketamine?!" Sherri laughed, having overheard their not-so-subtle conversation. "How the hell…" She laughed again, smacking the wall with her forearm and doubling over.

Chastity pointed to the pool table. "There was a guy hanging out down here who offered me some when I got here. I turned him down. I played around with party drugs in college. I don't really mess with that stuff anymore."

"Fuck. Ketamine?" Barrett muttered. "What do I do? Do I call an ambulance?"

"No," both women said in unison.

Sherri jovially added, "I don't… need this… kind of thing in the papers."

"She'll probably be fine." Chastity addressed Barrett. "When I tried it, it made me feel really happy, real euphoric. *Manic*, even." The word felt rotten on her tongue. "Then, later, it made me drowsy, and the next day, my roommate said I had been slurring a bit."

"So, she should be okay?" Barrett ran his hands through his hair.

"Yeah, I mean, it depends on how much she took. If it was just a little, her high will be really short. If she took a *lot*…"

"Jesus Christ. How could this have happened?" Barrett looked around.

"If she didn't take it willingly, she could have gotten dosed."

Barrett suddenly recalled the image of Sherri earlier in the evening, washing down the stuck ibuprofen tablets with the unknown contents of a solo cup seated on the edge of the pool table. All of the pieces clicked into place.

Barrett rushed over to the cup, lifted it, and pointed at it. "It was this. She only took a sip. I watched her. She had a headache, and I gave her some ibuprofen, and they got hung up in her throat."

"Oh, if it was just a sip, Sherri, you're gonna be fine. You just gotta ride it out, Honey, okay?"

Sherri giggled. "My *headache* is gone, at least."

Chastity laughed. "Yeah, I'll bet nothin' hurts right now, does it?"

Sherri shook her head. "Noooooope!"

Chastity shrugged. "That's why *I* took it. People told me it would make me feel happy and relax me a bit." She smoothed Sherri's hair softly, nurturing the woman. "I got just the thing for you. I saw you got that big ol' TV in your room." She took Sherri by the hand.

"Yeah?" Mrs. Nussbaum snickered, trying not to crack up again as she clutched Chastity's arm.

"You got streaming channels on that baby?"

"Yeah." Sherri snorted, face magenta from all the laughter.

"Let's get you nestled in where you're nice and safe and turn on some *Summer Love*. You ever seen it?"

"The reality show? God, no." Sherri shook her head and laughed as if the question was absolutely ridiculous. "My son watches all that garbage. I don't watch much TV."

"Oh, Sherri, trust me on this, you're gonna *hate* that you *love* it."

"That's a *great* idea." Barrett smiled, surprised by the new, caring side of Chastity he'd never seen before. "The two of you, go watch some trash TV. I'll finish up here and pop in to check on you when I'm finished."

"*Okayyyyyyy,*" Sherri sang, pressing against the wall for stability. Chastity tugged her away just in time for Sherri to miss a large, expensive-looking painting with her grabby hands.

Chastity looked over her shoulder at Barrett and smiled.

Barrett mouthed a grateful '*Thank you.*'

***

Three episodes of reality TV and one greasy, frozen pizza later, Sherri Nussbaum was sleeping off the last of the drugs in the Supima cotton sheets on her California king.

Barrett had scrubbed the lower level of the mansion spotless, leaving every conceivable surface disinfected and sparkling anew.

Quietly, he waved Chastity out of Sherri's chambers.

She followed Barrett back to his apartment, and they made their way upstairs. Barrett gathered bedding, and Chastity made up the couch with it.

"You killed it tonight," he said weakly, holding up his hand for a high-five.

Chastity beamed, excited to finally feel like she had genuinely done something right for a change. "Thanks. I didn't do much. Kinda just laid around and watched TV for the majority of it."

"You stayed calm when I wasn't. You took care of her. Probably showed her more kindness in one night than her family has in years."

"I don't know about all that."

"You were really sweet." He shrugged. "You'd make an amazing mom one day, I think." He quickly added, "I mean, if that was even something you ever wanted."

She smiled a little, but it was a sad one. She pounded the pillow against the armrest. "Yeah, maybe."

"I'm dead tired."

"Me too." She yawned, tucking herself in.

"I have tomorrow off. Get some shut-eye. We'll grab some breakfast and hit your place hard in the morning."

"You don't have to do that."

"I want to."

He padded off toward his bed and turned back for a moment. "Oh, and Aphrodite?"

"Yeah?" She sat up for a moment, cold nipples tenting the front of an oversized T-shirt that Barrett's grandmother bought as a show of support that read, '*I came. I saw. I cleaned.*'

"You make that lame-ass shirt look *really* damn good."

She blushed and slunk down beneath the covers. "Night, Adonis."

"Sleep well, Aphrodite."

19

Chastity awoke to the buzz of her phone. She shuffled off the couch and walked over to Smoky, petting the feline while peering into her green eyes.

She smoothed her own frazzled hair and sifted through a pile of clothes in the corner, pulling out a pair of basketball shorts. She slipped them on to cover her thong, cinched the drawstring, and threw on socks and shoes.

Barrett ambled out of the kitchen dressed similarly. In his hand, a pan of eggs sizzled.

He eyed Chastity up and down and then glanced down at his own attire.

"What is this? *Who Wore It Better*?"

Chastity groggily snickered. "I'd vote *you*." She gave him a sexy smile.

"Disagree." He shook his head. "How do you like your eggs?"

"Preferably out of the shell." That, she said with a straight face.

He shook his head and walked away, mumbling, "Smart ass…"

***

"Okay, please don't judge me by what you're about to see," Chastity pleaded, her jasmine perfume all Barrett could focus on as they stood outside the closed door to Apartment 208.

"How bad is it?"

"It's bad." She didn't hesitate. "Think about the last crack den you saw on *Intervention*. It's pretty much that."

Barrett took a dramatic inhalation and chewed his gum, pretending to prepare himself for the worst.

The flickering halogen bulb outside of her hallway suddenly stopped blinking, casting him in a steady beam. For a split second, she couldn't help but feel as if Barrett himself was, indeed, a light in all of her darkness.

He wagged a roll of trash bags at the door like a wand and said, "O*pen-ee-oh-sum!*"

"*You're not a wizard, Harry,*" Chastity said, mimicking Hagrid's voice.

"Surely, that would have worked at *Hogwarts*."

"Nerd."

He rolled his shoulders back. "I'm ready. Open it."

Chastity shifted the pail of cleaning supplies to her other hand and unlocked the door, throwing it wide open.

Barrett stepped in, eyes wide with momentary horror as he looked around. Then, his expression changed to one of confidence. "Oh, yeah. We *got* this."

"This is going to take forever." Her shoulders slumped.

"No way. Darlin', you're looking at a semi-trained amateur-professional."

Barrett's eyes studied the graffitied walls, the chaotic landscape of litter, and the paraphernalia that covered almost the entirety of the floor's surface in the living room.

"These are your new digs, huh?"

"Yup. *Home-crap-home*. I told you. I wasn't exaggerating."

"I see that. The upside is that this place is tiny. Shouldn't take that long to clean." He shrugged and looked at her. "The upside for me, personally, is that at this moment, my apartment looks *real good* in comparison."

She laughed. "Not *that* good."

Barrett wandered through the rooms, taking mental notes and figuring out an order of operations. He halted, peering down at something in the bathroom. "Is that a blow-up doll?"

Chastity sighed. "You saw that, huh?"

"Yeah… I kinda like it." He cocked his head to the side. "Kinda makes the place feel homey. You should put her by the door like a little Costco greeter."

***

Four hours later, the apartment was garbage-free and smelled of lemon-scented disinfectant.

"We'll get you some fresh paint and posters to cover the graffiti."

"Thank you for this. It already looks a million times better."

"You're welcome." He smiled. "Hey, maybe since you're starting out on a new adventure, *we* should start fresh, too."

She scrunched her brows, confused.

"I'll start." He stood up straight and smiled. "Hi, gorgeous. What's your name?"

He held out a hand.

She shook it reluctantly. "Hi, Barrett."

"No, dude, you don't know my name is *Barrett* yet. We're starting over."

She chuckled. "Fine. Hi… there. I'm… Chastity Erikson. And you are?"

"*Zeus.*" He was serious, expression never wavering.

Chastity chuckled and rolled her eyes. "I guess I deserved that one."

"It's fine. Women have every right to be cautious."

"Yeah, but I feel like most people are good. It's just the assholes that get the spotlight usually."

"Hmmm. True."

There was a long silence between them. Finally, Chastity looked up at him, nervous.

"I'm bipolar," she blurted.

She had no idea why she'd chosen then to say it. She just suddenly wanted to let him know. To warn him before he got too close.

Barrett just looked at her, stunned that something so deeply personal came out of her, seemingly out of nowhere.

"I mean," she cleared her throat. "I know you're being sweet and... you're trying to spend time with me... and you're doing these nice things, but before you think that this could be anything, I wanted to let you know."

"You say that like I'm trying to pressure you into dating." His tone was gentle. "Or like being bipolar is, like, somehow a deal-breaker."

"Well, *yeah*."

"It *isn't*." He shrugged. "And for the record, I'm not trying to pressure you into dating. I just... like being around you. You're not like anyone I've ever met before."

She didn't say a word.

"You're like this fast, beautiful, unbridled mare, unable to be broken by anyone. You've got this spirit that is…"

"Feral?"

"No." He laughed. "*Wild. Free.*"

"So you think I'm a *horse*?" she joked.

"I meant it as the highest possible compliment." He stepped toward her, cupping her face in his hands softly, aching to kiss her again. Deeply. Passionately.

He wanted to lay her on the stained carpet and fuck every last ounce of sadness straight out of her gorgeous body.

"You are not a horse. You are Aphrodite… goddess of sex and fake numbers."

Chastity laughed as a tear dribbled down her cheek. "You don't have to stick around now that you know. Everyone thinks I'm some kind of ticking time bomb. Who knows. Maybe I am."

"Give me more credit than that. One of my best friends in high school was bipolar. One of the nicest people I ever met. Sure, he had po-mouth. He was shit with money, and God *damn* was he impulsive, but he was also the biggest Teddy bear you'd ever meet."

"Are you guys still friends?" Chastity sniffled, sinking deeper into his cupped hands.

He stroked some rainbow-colored hair from her face, and his smile fell. She could tell from the pain in his expression that the friend in question was no longer alive.

"He would have probably really benefited from medication. Scientists didn't really know then what they know now. Now, it can be managed. Now, doctors know a *helluva* lot more about it."

She nodded.

"One or two?" he asked.

Chastity pulled away and put some of the solvents back in the pail. "I have… bipolar two. Just got the diagnosis about a month ago. I was going to a counselor at the college for a bit, and she sent me to a psychiatrist. Next thing you know, I have this label that I can't ever get rid of and a list of medications I'm supposed to take."

"Good."

"No. I won't do it." Chastity whipped her head to face him.

"Wait, what? Why not?"

"I'm not going to be some kind of *zombie* just to make everyone else's lives easier. Have you ever felt real mania, Barrett? They're… amazing. I want to savor every second of those highs that I *can*. I don't want to just float through life *emotionless*. I wouldn't be *me*."

Barrett stayed silent for a moment. Nodding.

"You knew I was weird, right? Well, now you know why."

He stepped toward her. "First of all, I like weird. No, I fucking *love* weird. Second, there is nothing wrong with being different. Look, my Gam-Gam always told me to think about people like a field of flowers. How boring it would be if they were all the same?"

She smiled a little. "Gam-Gam sounds pretty kick ass."

"She's the best. My parents died in a motorcycle accident when I was nine. Mom was riding on the back. Some lady in a soccer van didn't see them. Turned right into their lane. Clipped the front wheel and sent them over the edge of a raised part of the highway."

"Jesus. I'm so sorry."

"It was bad. Closed caskets for both of them. Still have a newspaper clipping somewhere of the mangled bike. Lady in the soccer van didn't even know what happened til the next day when the cops tracked her down."

"I'm so sorry, Barrett."

"My Gam-Gam and Gee-Paw raised my brother and I. For the most part, despite it all, she held it together. Stayed real positive. When I got older, I was the spitting image of my father, like a doppelganger almost. Gee-Paw had a hard time even looking at me. He died last year. Now it's just me, Gam-Gam, and my idiot brother, Dusty."

"What's Dusty like? I mean, besides being an idiot."

"He's older. Has a wife and two little girls who, *thankfully,* take after their mom. He owns a little house in the 'burbs with a Homeowner's Association that tells them how tall their grass is allowed to be. You've seen my place. That kind of structure is pretty much my worst nightmare."

She nodded, rubbing the sole of her untied Vans against a black stain on the carpet.

"I can't live a life like that. One where I feel dead and alive at the same time, living the same routine day after day, same co-workers telling you the same jokes, same meatloaf nights and taco Tuesdays, same ol' missionary position."

"Hey, don't you dare knock the missionary position…" she joked, moving closer to him.

"Speaking of missionary position…" He wrapped his hands softly around her waist.

She looked at her watch and purred, "Mmmm. No can do, handsome. I have to be at work in a half an hour."

"Okay." He backed away, fighting his smile and picking up two bags of trash by the door. "I should probably head out, too. Got a hot date tonight anyway."

"Oh yeah? What's ol' Gam-Gam making y'all for dinner?"

He laughed, shoulders sagging that she'd ruined the punchline. "She's been on a tilapia kick lately, if you *must* know."

Chastity smiled and headed toward the front door with his pail of supplies. It was only then that she noticed words written in Sharpie, '*There was once a hole here, but now it's gone.*' A red circle was drawn where a peephole would go.

Yup, the last tenants were definitely on some heavy drugs...

Chastity opened the door for him, took one of the bags out of his hands, and replaced it with the handle of his supply bucket. "I'll take this one down when I leave."

He shook his head and grinned. "*Stubborn.*"

"You know it."

He readjusted the bag and stared at her for a moment.

"Thank you for letting me crash at your place."

"No sweat."

"And thank you for... *all* of this." She motioned back to her now-empty apartment. "I wish I had some cash to give you."

"All good. I needed the practice. This was some great on-the-job training."

"Well, damn, I should have had you do this dressed as a slutty dark angel in a speedo and nipple clamps or something."

"Whatever you do, don't say that to my boss, or else it'll end up as a drop-down option on the website, for God's sake. Cleaning in feather wings... I take back what I said earlier... *that's* my damned *nightmare*."

Chastity laughed and rose to her tiptoes, wrapping her hands around the back of Barrett's neck to pull him down. She kissed him, long and soft, and he kissed back, cherishing the feel of her lips, her tongue.

She pulled away, eyes fixated on him for a moment before releasing his head from her hands. "Call me sometime?"

He started to walk down the hall, dragging the heavy sack on the carpet behind him. "No can do. Somebody lied about her number."

"*Fuck.*" She slapped her forehead. He was right.

"But," he chuckled, "you know where I live and how to find me."

"I do."

He grinned over his shoulder. "See you around, Aphrodite."

20

Barrett awakened from his nap to a chirping cell phone beneath his ribcage, tearing him from his dream about Chastity, naked and bent over her newly-scoured stove, being fucked from behind by him so hard that her screams of pleasure would surely have gotten her evicted.

He looked at his boner and groaned, snatching up the phone and looking at the row of text notifications, all from Will Jessup.

He struggled to focus on the tiny font, muscles aching from two straight days of scrubbing.

> **WILL: Nussbaum might be in love with you.**
>
> **WILL: She called and raved about you this morning. Said you did a hell of a job. She came by with a big cash tip. I'll give it to you tomorrow at the office.**

**WILL: Good work, man.
Proud of you. Thanks for
taking the emergency call.**

Barrett smiled, remembering the events of
the night before. He thought about Mrs.
Nussbaum's joyous laughter, the way Chastity
took care of the woman, the exchange of heated
glances and shy smiles as they cleaned together.

Then, he thought about the green and purple
smudges on her cheeks, about the boy
scrambling for his ugly ass shoes, about the torn
wrapper, and the look of embarrassment on
Chastity's face.

Jealousy twisted within him again.

That little piss-ant didn't deserve to be
inside of her. He wondered if the little twerp
made her cum anywhere as hard as Barrett had
just days before.

Before his mind could wind any further
down the rabbit hole, another text alert chimed.

**WILL: I called the bridal
boutique. They said you still
haven't had your tux fitted yet?
I told him there must have
been a mistake because my
best man wouldn't be putting
shit off until the last minute.**

Otherwise, I'd have to kick his ass.

Barrett winced.

They had not been mistaken. The more Ava had begged him to do it, the harder he seemed to procrastinate the task.

BARRETT: Your wedding is still six months away.

WILL: Ava's been hounding me about asking you. She's worried you're gonna keep putting it off. Please, dude. Just do it.

Barrett sighed and looked at his watch. It was still early enough in the afternoon to catch them before they closed.

BARRETT: I'll get it done today. Where do I go again?

WILL: Harmony. It's on Elm. I'll resend all the info now. Thanks a million. I know it's a drag, but it means a lot to Ava.

21

Harmony Bridal Boutique was a small family-owned shop a few miles away. Then again, in a town of thirteen thousand people, *everything* was only a few miles away.

The sun-faded imprint of the old *Radio Shack* logo shone behind the shop's new rose-pink ones. Female mannequins in bejeweled gowns crowded the tacky window display. Male mannequins stood in the other window wearing various suits and tuxedos that, to him, all looked fucking identical. They might as well be fashionable prison uniforms. Hell, he'd probably look better in inmate orange.

It *would* go well with his bronzed skin tone…

Maybe he should get Will to add an orange jumpsuit and ankle shackles to the website. Surely, there were some rich old ladies who would like to fantasize about being the domineering lady Warden bossing around prisoner zero-eight-two-nine-five.

As he pulled open the door, a sickening feeling washed over him. A blinding array of wedding attire stood all around him, overflowing into the area behind the counter at the center of the store, where a young clerk beamed at him.

"Hi! Can I help you?"

Barrett's skin crawled at all of the pastels, lace, and chiffon as he approached her.

"Hi, yes, you can." Barrett looked around at the walls, striped with white gowns and black suits like some bizarre piano he would never be equipped to play.

"I'm supposed to get fitted for my tux. The groom said to come here. Said it would be under the Jessup-Quinn account."

"No problem. I'm Marcy. I'll be helping you today. We will get you measured in a jiff."

"Great."

The clerk flipped through a massive binder, one that had to weigh a good fifteen pounds. "Are you family or a member of the party?"

"Bridal party." He smiled. "Best man, actually."

"Oh, congratulations. This is such a fun time for you." Marcy peered at him with steel-blue eyes. Something about her seemed hopeful and innocent, putting him at ease. She didn't seem like a pressuring menace, more like a sickeningly sweet helping hand.

"Sure." He cracked half a smile. "I'll take your word for it."

He glanced to his right. At a short ten-foot-long rack, the boutique had a lingerie display. There were filthy snow-white numbers, some with bows attached. There were fishnet body stockings, bralettes, garters, panty sets, and lacy negligees galore. He couldn't help but imagine Chastity's body in some of them as Marcy penciled some things into the book.

Moments later, a door swung open behind him, and a gaggle of women stepped out of a room with a platform and a wall of mirrors. The women were clucking excitedly about the bride, a female in the center that they were all fawning over.

Then, without warning, a woman came out of the room behind them with a wedding gown raised over her head to keep it off the floor. She hollered to Marcy, and he recognized the voice immediately. It sent a shock straight through him.

"She said 'Yes' to the dress, Marcy!" Chastity sang.

Barrett's eyes widened as she came into view, and for a split second, he was in that back room with her in his mind, holding her naked body to his, standing tall on the platform, cupped hands pulling on her pierced nipples, making her watch the pleasure in her own face as he entered her inviting warmth from behind.

"Barrett!" Chastity's excited voice was like music in his ears. She was dressed nicely in a simple black suit top, white blouse, and a black skirt that hugged her delicious figure like it had been made just for her. Her rainbow hair was twisted into a messy updo.

She jogged toward him, holding the giant, plastic-shrouded pile of fabric like a dying person laid across the crooks of her arms.

"Long time no see. It's been like... what? Three hours?"

Barrett laughed. "You said you worked at a boutique. I should have put two-and-two together. I feel like an idiot."

"No! Don't." She leaned up and gave him a simple peck on the cheek.

Marcy's eyes darted to the two of them, watching the interaction carefully. Finally, she whispered. "Oh. Is *he* why you were thirty minutes late today?"

Chastity's smile vanished. "No. I told you. I had to talk to the super. I didn't have any hot water. And trust me, after that party, I went to last night, a shower was *mandatory*."

Marcy nodded and wrote more things in her giant tome. "Alright. Mr. Andrews, right?"

"That's correct. How did you know?"

"You're the last one from your bridal party to be fitted. It was just process of elimination.

Follow me. I'll have you look through our catalog of ties and pocket squares while Chastity gets ready to take your measurements."

He followed Marcy to a corner in the back, settling into a simple black leather armchair with a book the size of *War and Peace* in his lap. He flipped through endless pages of what seemed like the same necktie over and over with subtle differences he couldn't see. He flipped past the bow ties completely to the pocket square section, starting with a horrendous vomit-green paisley one that made him want to gag.

He didn't even know the colors of Will and Ava's wedding, nor did he care.

"Can't I just do a black pocket square?" He asked no one in particular. "Doesn't black go with, like, everything?"

A few minutes later, Chastity stood by the door to the room in the back. "Mr. Andrews!" She beckoned him over with a finger.

He grinned.

The small room was fairly bare with white walls and bright, diffused tube lights in every corner, giving the medium-sized room a Heaven-type vibe. Barrett suddenly regretted leaving his sunglasses in the car.

A foot-tall white, wooden platform sat in the middle. A small changing room jutted out from one corner, its door open wide, unloved wedding gowns hanging on a hook inside. In front of the platform sat a row of stools and a wall of mirrors butted against each other like some kind of dance studio. In another corner, there was a beverage cart with an empty bottle of cheap champagne, an opened can of seltzer water, and several plastic drink flutes.

"Jesus, it's so bright here. These on a dimmer at all?" He squinted while his eyes adjusted.

"Afraid not," she smiled, shutting the door and pulling the measuring tape from around the back of her neck. "Can I have you stand on the platform for me, Sir?"

"Oh, Jesus." His eyes fluttered. "Girl, keep calling me *'Sir,'* and we are going to have a real *problem* here."

She tried to hide her smile but failed miserably. "So you've taken to stalking now, huh?"

"What can I say? I just can't get enough of you." He touched her lip and let his finger trail down her chin, her neck, softly teasing the skin below her throat.

"Sir, I need you to strip down to your underwear so that I can get accurate measurements for your tux."

"What if I'm not wearing any?" he asked, face dead-serious.

"I can see if Marcy has a pair of boxers out there for purchase."

"Alright, you called my bluff." He stripped out of his boot-cut jeans, revealing a pair of briefs in an American flag design. "I'm sure this is already going to cost a fortune. No sense piling on more expenses."

Chastity toyed with her measuring tape.

"You know I'm living on a *maid's* salary, right?"

"Poor baby." She grinned. "Though, I hear all the horny old broads in Jackson tip mighty fine if you give 'em a little *show* while you clean. Just food for thought."

She winked, and Barrett thought his bare knees might buckle for a split second.

Chastity looked down at his underwear. "Mmmm. America the beautiful."

Barrett smiled at the ceiling. "You're already having *way* too much fun with this."

"Sir, for the most accurate measurements, I'm gonna have to ask you to lose the shirt, too."

"You're getting a little pushy." He looked down at the tape in her hands. "Just remember when you start measuring, not everything is going to be accurate. It's chilly in here."

She burst into a laugh and then grabbed one of the stools along the wall and placed it on the platform beside him.

He held his muscular arms out, the pinnacle of male perfection. Like Da Vinci's *Vitruvian Man.* She pulled a small notepad and pencil out of a lace-covered bin above the door and set the items atop the stool. Quietly, she measured around the widest part of his chest, making sure to brush her hands against his hardened pecs. She scribbled the number down on a pad.

As a charged silence fell between them, her hands grazing various parts of his body, she measured his hips, wrists, and biceps.

As she measured his shoulders, she tiptoed up and nuzzled her nose against the skin near the back of his neck, hot breath against him as she dragged her lips across a few inches of his skin.

He moaned a little, softly. "You know your boss is going to come in here and see you harassing the customers."

"I'd shudder to think about what would happen if she saw me do this. Her father would fire my ass in a heartbeat."

Chastity's hand slid around the front of his waist, down along the hard cut of his abdomen, behind the flag, deep into his briefs. He moaned again as she massaged his cock, strengthening his already-growing erection.

"*Jesus Christ,*" he whispered into the ether.

Her hand retracted, and he felt the tape press from his neck to the top of his underwear before she scribbled more numbers on the pad.

She measured his neck, placing soft kisses down his spine as she did. Barrett's flag was at full mast, underwear tented from his arousal.

She measured around his waist and hips, writing quickly.

"Can I have you turn around, please, S*ir*?" She waited a moment. "I have to get your *inseam*."

"Gladly," he said, barely finding the voice to speak as he spun in place to face her.

He craned his neck down and kissed her hard, stealing the breath from her lungs when he did. He pulled her face against his, tongue fierce and probing. He grabbed the lapels of her blazer and yanked it halfway down her arms, limiting her arm movements like handcuffs, kissing the tops of her breasts with fervor.

"Does that door have a lock," he muttered between kisses.

"No," she panted, eyeing the handle. Marcy could walk in at any moment and see them like this. She closed her eyes, enjoying the feel of his lips on her skin.

Seconds later, her jacket was off, blouse tugged over her head, bra unsnapped in a lump on the white platform, one of her pierced nipples in his hot mouth.

She started to moan, but he clasped a hand over her mouth to silence her. His lips unlatched from her breast, and he quietly growled in her ear. "You don't want Marcy to hear us, now do you?"

She shook her head, mouth still silenced by his palm. He plunged his other hand beneath the waistband of her skirt, beneath her panties, slipping his middle finger through her folds, feeling the soaked opening beneath.

"*God damn, Aphrodite.*"

She bit his palm softly, eyes slits at the sensation of his curled finger hooking up inside of her.

"You should *measure my inseam.*" He nodded down to his cock, hard as stone between their bodies.

She pulled away and smiled, lowering to her knees. She slowly tugged his underwear down to his thighs.

She looked up at him, amber eyes begging to taste him. He nodded, and she took him into her mouth, slipping her lips around and taking him deep into the back of her throat.

Barrett wanted to scream, biting his own fist to stay quiet. He stared down at her breasts, pierced and full, jiggling as she bobbed, never once choking despite how deep she could take him.

Pressure building, he pulled away, grabbed her by the armpits, and pulled her to her feet. He slapped away the notepad, flinging it into the corner and resting his ass on the cold, bare wood of the stool. He grabbed at her skirt, roughly jerking it up until the bottom was at her rib cage. He snatched her up by her waist, arms powerful and unyielding.

He wanted her.

Now.

"*Fuck, my wallet… a condom,*" he panted.

"I'll take a Plan B tomorrow."

The 'O' sound hadn't even come out of her mouth before he lifted her onto his lap. She clung to him, bare ass on undeniable display for anyone who dared to come through the unlocked door.

In one deft motion, he slid her lace thong to the side and drove her soaking-wet pussy down onto his cock.

She gasped.

"*Shhhhhh.*" He clutched her close by her rainbow hair, wrenching her toward his and pushing her down further on his dick by it until he was as deep as he could possibly be inside of her.

He kissed her, rocking her hips up and down upon his own with strong hands, pounding her pelvis down against him with raw aggression. She ground against him, desperate for friction, hand sliding down between them to play with her clit.

He groaned quietly in her ear. *"Fuck, Aphrodite. You're gonna make me cum."*

She kissed him hard, biting his bottom lip so roughly that he thought it might bleed. Even as he let her go, she pounded her pelvis against him harder, legs trembling.

Finally, she thrashed, flinging her head back, arching her spine, body shuddering in his lap.

He closed his eyes, squeezed both of her ass cheeks hard in his hands, and plunged up into her faster for his own release. He seized, arched feet shaking against the ground like the hooves of an unsteady fawn. Her hand slipped over his mouth. He ground his teeth tight, neck taut, veins popping as he came.

***

"Measurements are all set, Marcy. I'll get these in the book, and our in-house tailor will get to work on it, Mr. Andrews," Chastity said, nervously smoothing the fallen locks of rainbow hair coming out of the back of her bun.

"Thank you, Ms. Erikson. I was really worried that this was going to be an awful drag, but I must say, you made that a *very* pleasant experience."

Barrett turned toward Marcy at the desk and pointed to Chastity as she retreated back into the room with the platform.

"Top-notch customer service. If you guys have a questionnaire, I'd be happy to fill one out. I'm a very satisfied customer."

Marcy seemed suspicious but returned her eyes to her paperwork. "I'm glad to hear it, Mr. Andrews. I'm sure the owner will be pleased to hear that."

"We all set here?" Barrett tapped his fingers nervously on the counter, waiting for the girl to clear him to leave.

"Not quite. Just going through a few things to make sure we put the right order in. It looks like the Jessups picked pearl, coal, and ruby as their theme. Groomsmen all have pearl shirts, and it seems Ava left us a note here to put you in a ruby shirt with a pearl tie and pocket square."

"It's weird. I play dress up for my main job, and it doesn't feel like nearly as much of a chore as all of this wedding stuff?"

"Oh yeah? What do you do?" She never looked up.

Barrett froze for a second, unsure how to answer it. His mind raced through several of his barely-there outfits during the last few days, and he suddenly felt ashamed of his new vocation.

"I… run… a playhouse. Outside of town," he lied. "Like, *wayyy* outside of town. We do a lot of Shakespeare. Boring stuff."

That got her attention. "Oh, *huge* thespian here."

"That's awesome. Love you who love."

She quirked an eyebrow at him and then continued, "I *love* Shakespeare. I actually was in *Romeo and Juliet* in high school."

"Oh, no way." His eyes refused to blink as he mentally shit himself. "I'll bet you were a top-notch Juliet."

Her eyes met his, full of disappointment. "I was Lady Capulet, actually."

"Bummer." He looked around, eager to end the conversation.

"Yeah, and in *Midsummer*, I was—"

"Any way we could wrap this up? We've got auditions this afternoon, and it's a long, loooong drive."

"Ooooh, whatcha casting for this time? Othello?"

"Hamlet," he said. It was the only other Shakespearean play he could name.

"Oooooh, I love Hamlet. '*To be, or not to be. That is the question.*'"

"Actually, the question is, 'Are we all good here?'"

She frowned and scribbled something else down. "Yes, we're all set. You can pay for the suit when you come back for your fitting. We will give you a call when it's ready."

"How much is this gonna run me?"

"Suit, shirt, pocket square, and tie…" She turned away, furiously clicking her middle finger against an old-school calculator, tallying up the expenses. "It'll be $317.83."

"Jesus Christ, you have it in your book that I'm only *renting* it, right?"

22

A week of cleaning and painting after work transformed Chastity's apartment from a hideous meth den to an actual livable space.

She adjusted her position on her new futon, one that served both as a bed for her and a couch for future guests. It was cheap, and she wanted more, but for now, it would have to do if she didn't want to sleep in a sleeping bag on the floor. She'd even gotten the delivery men to bring it upstairs and unbox the thing for her with some casual flirting and feminine wiles.

On the futon, her laptop, a thin one sporting a bumper sticker from the college she'd recently flunked out of, was open to the streaming season finale of *Summer Love*. A crying woman stormed out of the camera's view, and the show cut to a commercial break.

Chastity leaned back and looked around. She craved an exciting distraction. She wanted to be near fun people. Pretending that everything was okay while socializing made her feel like it actually *was okay*, even if only temporarily.

Something felt off in her body, as though the joy had slowly been draining from her like a tire's slow leak. The manic high when she was kicked out of her college dorm had faded, and now, something empty and hollow remained.

Somewhere, deep down, she knew it would pass. *It always did.* The depressive lows would once again be replaced by the manic highs, and everything would feel great again.

No matter how much yoga, deep breathing, and *gratitude exercises* her psychiatrist had suggested, nothing ever *made* the low subside. It felt like an exercise in futility every time she pulled out her journal to get her thoughts on paper.

Her stomach's empty growl was followed by her phone's text notification.

RACHEL: Hey girl! Heard today you were back in town. What the fuck? Why haven't you hit me up? I'd have bought you a coffee, slut.

She hadn't heard from Rachel Magnuson in nearly a year. They were ships in the night, always missing each other for various reasons.

In high school, Rachel had always been genuine and fun. She also had a stunning complexion and a honking laugh that was infectious. Over the past half-decade, Rachel had found immense satisfaction in being one of Jackson's premiere exotic dancers.

Chastity smiled down at her phone.

> **CHASTITY: Holy shit. Blast from the fuckin' past. How the hell are you?**

> **RACHEL: Shit's fire. I'm working down at The Thirsty Rancher now.**

> **CHASTITY: Is that a new gentleman's club? I feel like college threw me out of the loop on all these new places popping up.**

> **RACHEL: Ain't no gentlemen there, lemme tell ya. But yeah! Not sure if you heard, but *The Firehose* burned down last year. Bitches overloaded the wiring in the dressing room, and the whole fucking place went up like a tinderbox.**

CHASTITY: Oh shit! Did everyone make it out okay?

RACHEL: Everyone's fine. New joint is way cooler, though. It's past the Homewood Suites on the way up toward Beaver Creek.

CHASTITY: Hahaha. Beaver Creek. How fitting.

RACHEL: LOL. I love it there. You walk out the door at the end of a shift, and it's just Tetons for days.

CHASTITY: Sounds pretty! Damn, it's been forever. We should hang out sometime. I miss you, bitch.

RACHEL: How about now? Bunch of us ladies got invited to a costume party down in South Park. You should throw something on and come. Heard a rumor that it's gonna be a sausage fest. Pretty girl like

you could have your pick of the litter.

RACHEL: It's an open bar.

Free booze, rough sex, and a night out of the apartment seemed like an ideal way to rid Chastity of all boredom and intrusive thoughts. She loved *Summer Love*, but she'd seen this entire season three times already. Soon, she'd be able to recite it along with the show.

Her stomach growled again. She imagined the party, and her mind drifted to countertops full of cheese plates and salami. She could go for a beer, a good lay, or a bag of Doritos all the same.

CHASTITY: Do you have a costume I could borrow?

RACHEL: Sure! But it's gonna be skanky and covered in glitter.

CHASTITY: Perfect. Send me your address. I'll head over now and get changed.

23

Chastity slipped out of Rachel's sedan onto the frost-stiff dead grass. The late spring night still had a bite to it. Fogged breath oozed from their cherry-red lipstick-covered mouths. Rachel was dressed like a sexy feline. It was as if she were the lead actor in a strip club presentation of the musical *CATS*.

Chastity wore a *Little Red Riding Hood* get-up. She donned a short, red cloak, hem so high up her thighs it barely covered her rear. Cleavage peeked out over the top of her ruffled, white sleeveless blouse, cinched at the waist by a corset. Red thigh-highs were held in place by garters. A pair of worn, white cowboy boots met them in the middle of her shin.

Flickering lights glinted through the worn slats on the side of the massive barn, coaxing the women in from the stirred-up dust of the dirt parking lot.

Several men laughed at the entrance of the barn door, each with a bottle of beer in their hands. As Chastity and Rachel approached, the men couldn't keep their eyes off them. Chastity smiled bashfully at the much-needed attention.

Inside the barn, a wild, costumed party was in full swing. The interior was rustic. Streamers draped from the center of the ceiling to the walls. A twirling golden party light hung on a chain from the middle, spinning on a motor like a disco ball. The dirt floor was hard from the cold and packed tight from the foot traffic. Hay bales provided seating along the walls, and picnic tables were scattered along one side. In the middle, people line danced to a country song that blared from mounted speakers. Body heat and drunken laughter filled the space.

Against the back wall, a bartender in a Zorro mask noisily shook a cocktail shaker.

"Oooh. I see a bar. Want something?" Chastity asked.

"Nah, I'm gonna split off. Do a round. See what's good. Try to do some recon on where the best beefcake is at."

Chastity laughed, blew Rachel a kiss, and made her way through the costumed horde toward the bar. Stools made of halved whiskey barrels with wooden legs lined a bar inhabited by men in a variety of costumes.

She leaned over the worn wood to flirt with the bartender. Several of the men behind her eyed the bottom bit of her bare ass cheeks, now visible below the cape's edge.

"Eyes forward if you wanna keep them in your fucking heads," a familiar voice growled, a blanket threat to all the gawking patrons.

Chastity turned in time to see the men averting their gazes. She twisted toward the source of the stern order and felt a smile break out across her lips despite her desire to keep it stifled.

Barrett Andrews.

Small world.

Even smaller town…

There he stood, six-foot-four-inches of muscled physique in a leather jacket, tight black jeans, and white tee, hair slicked.

"Let me guess… Danny Zuko?" She smirked.

"Oddly enough, I came straight from work. I just cleaned a lady's *oven* in this. Client was obsessed with *Grease*. She stood around watching me in a *poodle* skirt."

"No, she didn't."

"I shit you not!" he exclaimed.

"In retrospect, Little Red, I should've come as a *wolf* because, God damn, you look *good enough to eat.*"

Heat bloomed in her belly when his eyes lingered on her.

"Can I buy you a drink?" he asked.

"*It's an open bar, Stud*," she said mockingly in the voice of Olivia-Newton. "They're free."

He put his hands up as if to say, 'Well, excuse me.'

Chastity waved at the bartender. A few feet away, a man dressed in a deer onesie complete with felt antlers stared at her ass from his seat at the bar.

Seeing this, Barrett glared at him, teeth clenched. When their eyes met, Barrett shook his head. The deer tipped his bottle at Barrett and smiled wickedly.

Chastity leaned over the counter again, giggling with the bartender as he poured her a drink. The way her cloak bared the bottom of her shapely ass, exposing the thin strip of solid red thong beneath, made Barrett's cock stiffen.

"You here with anyone?" Barrett asked, leaning in.

"This chick, Rachel. She's around her someplace. How about you? You got a date?"

"Nope." Barrett slicked the sides of his hairdo. "Zuko rides solo."

"How'd you even hear about this? Aren't you a little *old* for these kinds of parties?"

"Ouch!" He clutched at his heart. "Shots fired. Organ pierced. Man down." Barrett took a fresh beer from behind the counter, laid it against the edge of the bar, and slammed his fist down, sending the cap flying into the hay behind the bar. "Jesus, Aphrodite. I'm only in my *thirties*."

"*Mid*-thirties." Chastity snagged one of the whiskey barrel stools beside him, wincing as the cold wood touched her bare behind. "I was wondering how long it would be before I got to see you again."

"I see you're all set." The bartender eyed the beer in Barrett's hand, frustrated.

"You were busy. I thought I'd do you a solid. Can I also get two fingers of whiskey, please?"

The bartender nodded and put Chastity's drink in front of her. "One long island, ma'am."

"Thank you." Chastity grabbed the beverage and turned to face Barrett.

A moment later, a glass with an inch of amber liquor was plopped in front of him. Barrett shoved a five-dollar bill in the man's tip pitcher and slammed the whiskey, sliding the empty glass back and chasing it down with a swig of beer.

Barrett's eyes skimmed every delicious inch of Chastity's exposed skin. "I had a fantasy like this once."

Chastity chuckled. "I'll bet you did."

Barrett leaned in closer, wanting nothing more than to slip his hand between her thighs and massage the sensitive spot between them right here in public as oblivious people mingled about.

"Who throws a costume party in a barn here in the spring? This is so bizarre."

"I think it's sweet," Barrett said.

"You think *what's* sweet?"

"You don't know what this is for?"

She shook her head.

"City councilman renewed his vows. His wife apparently has pretty crippling social anxiety. Said being in costume is just about the only way she feels comfortable enough to be around people. So he organized this so they can celebrate, and she won't stand out like a turd in a punch bowl."

"Oh my God, that's really nice," Chastity cooed.

"That's what love is *supposed* to look like. Being there for someone despite their flaws. You didn't know that?"

Chastity smiled at the sentiment, warming at the thought of one day finding someone to accept her, diagnosis and all.

"No," she said, shaking her head. "I don't know what I thought this was. I heard open bar, and I just kinda jumped at the invite."

Barrett laughed at that.

"Wait, how the hell do *you* know all that?"

Barrett used the neck of his beer to point to a man dressed head-to-toe in a hot dog costume. "See the wiener?"

Chastity snickered at the question and sucked down more of her drink through the straw.

"His wife is a bottle of mustard. She's runnin' around somewhere here. She's besties with the councilman. Got the invite from her. Mrs. Mustard is a client."

"No shit?"

"Yeah. Monday, she had me clean in a full Delta pilot outfit. Guess back in the day, she was a flight attendant. She said when she was younger, she met Mr. Weiner over there and couldn't keep her hands off him. She's got a thing for the uniform now, I guess."

"Wild." She shook her head. "Does Mr. Weiner know?"

"About what? That I come to dust her vents wearing only baby oil and half a pilot's uniform?"

"Yeah."

"Who do you think signs my *checks*?"

"No wayyyyy."

"Yes, way. He wants a spotless house, and he wants to see his wife happy. As long as I keep my dick in my pants, he's fine with it."

Barrett pointed to a woman in the middle of a line dance. She was beaming in her fringe shirt and rhinestone studded pants with a cowboy hat on her head.

"Seems like the councilman's wife is havin' a ball."

Chastity grinned at Barrett.

"What?"

"You just have a handsome smile. That's all."

"You think so?"

Chastity shook her head. "Ugh, I'm making your massive head bigger, aren't I? Forget I said anything."

Barrett placed his hand on her knee and stroked it gently with his thumb. "When it comes to you, Aphrodite, I forget nothing."

The music changed, and the line dancers dispersed.

"Well, then you surely remember how well I dance."

"That I do." He stood, extending his hand to her.

She placed her still-half-full glass on the bar and followed Barrett to the dance floor. Peeling back her red hood, Chastity's hand slipped into his. He pulled her body flush against him, and they gently swayed to the slow tempo with a slight embarrassment neither had expected.

Neither said a word, exchanging only glances, letting their bodies move together in harmony once again.

Finally, Barrett spoke.

"What is this?"

"I think it might be Keith Urban," she mumbled.

"No. What is *this*? This *thing* between us. I can't seem to stay away from you," he said softly enough that only she could hear. "Or am I the only one feeling it?"

She shook her head, deep orange eyes peering into his soul. "It's not just you. I feel it, too."

She laid her head against his shoulder and swayed for a while. As the song waned, Barrett's body stiffened, freezing in place as others moved about.

"What's wrong?" Chastity looked up at his face, his eyes locked on something over her shoulder.

"Excuse me," he said sternly, pulling his body from hers and stalking angrily back to the bar. The absence of his body left chilled air in his wake.

From the middle of the dance floor, she watched as Barrett tugged the man in a deer onesie to his feet.

"What the fuck is wrong with you?" She heard Barrett's angered voice cutting through all the commotion, and he pointed to Chastity's drink at the bar.

The deer gave a snide smile and said something back that set Barrett off. Barrett punched the deer so hard that the man in the onesie collapsed to the ground like a rag doll.

Chastity gasped, along with several others around her. Two men leaped off their stools, holding Barrett back from going at the deer for another punch.

Barrett shook the men off of him and bolted away, exiting through the barn door to the parking lot.

Chastity raced out the door, confused and stunned. "Barrett! What the hell just happened in there?"

"That fucking asshole slipped something in your drink!"

He was livid, pacing. He stopped in the middle of the parking lot and ran his hands through his gelled black hair.

"Wait, he *what*? You *saw* him?"

"Yes! That's why I knocked him the fuck out! Fucking *creep*. I *knew* I didn't like the way he was looking at you."

Chastity was conflicted between the insatiable urge to either violently kiss or shake him.

"You could have just told me. We could have called the cops. You can't just go around punching people!"

"I know, I know! This isn't my first rodeo. Keeping my cool around fuck-heads is *not* my strong suit." He groaned. "I'm sorry if I embarrassed you, but I am *not* sorry I laid that dude out."

Whirling red-and-blue strobes flicked across Barrett's hardened features as a black Jackson patrol car slid quickly into the gravel lot, stones crunching like snow beneath the tires.

Barrett winced. "Aww, *goddammit*. Not *again*!"

24

"You get that costume from a Spirit Halloween? Or did you just have all the parts lyin' around?" John Ridgeway asked.

"Your mom actually gave it to me as a 'Thank you' gift last time I banged her brains out."

"Gross. My mother is eighty-nine.."

Barrett laughed. "I know. She's ancient. Feel like she knew the Apostles first-hand, but, hey, old ladies need love, too."

"Well, that makes what I'm about to tell you even more awkward, then." He sighed. "Barrett, I'm actually your father."

Barrett burst into laughter, and the officer's lips curled up into a smile.

"Oh, shut the fuck up, John." Barrett's face grew serious. "Can I go home yet?"

"Well. You see, this wasn't a little bar fight at *The Alibi*. You committed battery in front of a room full'a Jackson big-wigs. You're making it really goddamn hard to keep letting this stuff slide, man."

"John, I'm sorry. He just…"

"We know." John jingled the keys in his pocket before opening Barrett's cell door. "The guy you dropped like a sack of potatoes was the councilman's *son*. When your girl told him *why* you punched him, they agreed to drop the charges, probably to avoid some bad press."

Barrett felt his head go light when John said the words '*your girl.*' They felt good to hear. Like there was somehow a person in this world that was *his*.

"She's waitin' in the lobby. Told us about the kid trying to roofie her. But consider the *horseshoes* you had stuck up in your ass officially *removed*, Barrett. Make sure that's your last brawl. Next time, I *promise* you, you won't be so lucky."

Barrett nodded and held his hand out. "You have my word, John."

The officer's hand shook his with enough force to make Barrett grunt in pain. "Seriously. No more bullshit. Stay outta trouble."

John led Barrett out to the lobby. The door to the intake area closed behind them with a jarring slam.

Chastity and Rachel stood up in unison. He smiled at Chastity, raced to her, and clutched her in his arms, hugging her tightly. He kissed the top of her bright-colored head and pulled away.

"This is my friend, Rachel. We came together, so I had to have her…" Chastity trailed off, smiling at Barrett.

"Thanks for teaching that dick a lesson," Rachel said, her long brown hair flowing over her skintight spandex outfit with heels that made her almost as tall as Barrett. He silently wondered how she could walk in those things.

"I wasn't just gonna stand around and do nothing."

"*Next time* you will," John said, butting in from the windowed area to the back.

Chastity tilted up her head, pressed a kiss to Barrett's lips, and held it, breathing in the smell of his woody cologne on his skin. She gripped his white T-shirt and pulled him closer.

"Soooo, am I good to go here?" Rachel said, pointing to the front door anxiously.

Barrett pulled away and smiled, Little Red's lipstick all over his mouth. "Yes, ma'am. I'll get her home safely."

***

The *Rabbit Run* lot was nearly full. The ride back had been full of topical chatter about the costume party and the woman working intake at the jail who had a mustache that could rival any man's.

Barrett opened the Jeep's door and helped her out. Chastity stared up at the stars and laughed quietly.

Barrett leaned against the SUV, looking down at her with a look of humored confusion. "Everything alright?"

"Oh." She tried to quell the laughter. "I'm terrified that I almost got roofied tonight. But I'm laughing because of the look that man gave you right before you clobbered him," she giggled, "It was *literally* like... *deer in the headlights.*"

Barrett chuckled, eyes skimming over the lines of her body, nearly a silhouette against the mountains, skin washed pale by the moon. Her jasmine perfume tickled at his nose.

Her eyes met his, body inching toward him until their lips met again, tongues alive and melding. She leaned against him, gripping her fingers into his tee, dragging him closer.

Together, they were candles, dancing in the shadows of night, desperately seeking to sustain their flames through the burning heat of one another.

He groaned as she sucked his bottom lip between her teeth and bit down ever-so-gently.

He pressed his hard length against her thigh, hands caressing the bare skin of her ass below her costume. She reached down and massaged the bulge between his legs. His fingers roamed higher, exposing more of her skin to the frigid night air.

Suddenly, a pair of headlights flicked on behind them, bathing them in blinding light. Barrett's hand retreated, not needing a public indecency charge to add to his list of the night's offenses. Finally, the vehicle switched to its low beams and passed them to exit the lot.

Barrett grinned, lips red from the remnants of her makeup.

"You want to come upstairs for a bit?"

He looked at his watch. "I wish I could, but as of right now, if I go straight home, I will get *maybe* three and a half hours of sleep before I have to be at a client's house way out on 191."

"*Damn.*" She smoothed the short front of her outfit, hand continuing down to a spot between her thighs. "Guess I'll just have to dream of you, then."

He groaned, dick swelling at the thought of Chastity masturbating to a mental image of him beneath her covers.

"Maybe this is the part where you give me your real number."

She shrugged. "Or… maybe this is the part where you ask me out on a proper date."

Barrett laughed, shoving his hands in his pockets to distract from the tented fabric his erection was creating. "This is officially the hardest I have ever worked for a girl's number."

"Good." She smirked.

"What do you like to do?" He grinned. "Other than rock a man's world in the bedroom, I mean."

She smiled. "Pretty much anything that gets me out of the apartment. I'm not picky."

"Hmmm. We should do something fun. Would you care to accompany me to… mini-golf?"

"Hmmmm," Chastity hummed, thinking about it. "You should know now that I am competitive."

"Good. Getting to watch you get all flustered as a bunch of rando kids cheer me on for beating you? Sounds like a fun way to spend an afternoon."

"You have a lot of confidence for a man who is about to get his ass kicked at putt-putt."

"Trust me, I'm aware you're probably going to be good. You've already proven you've got incredible ball-handling skills."

That made her laugh loudly, the sound of which warmed Barrett's heart.

He opened the driver's door of the Jeep and put a foot on the mat. "Check your work schedule and just text me what day is good for….

ohhhhhh, you can't. Can you?" He forced his face into a smug frown.

She held her hand out. "Fine! Give me the damn phone."

"Yessssss." Barrett handed his phone to her, and she turned and whirled her arm, pretending she was going to chuck it into the nearby bushes. His stomach flipped at the sight of it.

"I'm kidding." She giggled, swiped the screen, and changed the fake number to her real one in his contacts list before handing it back.

He shook it at her. "Now, young lady, don't be sending me any photos of those piercings. That would be just... *awful*," he joked. "No pictures of the rest of you either, you hear me? No shower pics... nothing in lingerie. That would be... you know... a real *travesty*."

"A travesty. Of course. So crotch shots are out, too, then, I suppose."

He looked away, pounded a fist on the roof of the Jeep, and then looked back at her.

"You are something special," he finally said with a smile so bright and charming that Chastity wanted to swoon.

"Now buzz off before my landlord sees I'm attracting all of Jackson's riff-raff to her property," she said, turning around and wrapping her shoulders in the red cape in such a way that it flashed a few inches of the bottom of her bare ass to him.

"Jesus Christ," he muttered as he settled in the SUV. "Girl's gonna be the death of me."

25

Barrett looked out of the panoramic window at the behemoth Grand Tetons surrounding Jackson Lake. It wasn't often he'd gotten this far north, but every time he did, the view astounded him. Every time he laid eyes on the snowy peaks and lush meadows around the body of water, it felt like the first time.

Jackson Hole was stunning, he had to admit. He imagined other cities would have their appeal, too. He'd grown eager to venture elsewhere, always imagining extended trips to rainy London and the sweltering Florida Keys. Hell, even *Nebraska* would be a change of scenery.

Growing up in Jackson Hole, he watched the small picturesque town grow with him. But lately, it felt... *too* small. The surrounding mountains used to feel like a protective shield against the outside world, but now it felt more like a container. The same faces passed by him at the grocery store, at church service, at the honky tonk, at the gym.

He felt suffocated. Like he was in the film *Groundhog's Day*, forced to relive the same day with the same people over and over again.

Barrett stared through fake wire-rimmed glasses as prismatic lights from the front door's slotted windows dappled the dusty entryway in front of him. He wore a white long-sleeve shirt unbuttoned halfway down his chest, sleeves rolled to his elbows. Tight, pressed slacks clung to the curves of his ass.

The *Unscrupulous Professor* costume wasn't the most comfortable thing to clean in and probably provided the most skin coverage of all of the costumes, but for the last two hours, this particular client, Mrs. Walton, looked like she was about to have a hands-free orgasm just watching *Professor Anderson* wipe her fixtures down.

After the sconce in front of him was sparkling, he turned to her. "Was that the last one?"

"It was," she said firmly. "I still have you for another hour, though." Her sultry tone was about as subtle as a sledgehammer. "How about you teach me a little *lesson*, say, in the bedroom, Professor?"

He laughed nervously, unsure what to say. Had he not been on thin ice with Will and Ava or enamored by his rainbow-haired Aphrodite, old

Barrett would have had his clothes off by now, smacking this woman's ass implants and making her deep-throat his dick as penance for making *The Professor* stay late to supervise her detention.

New Barrett wanted to keep his job, one that was already paying almost triple what he'd been paid to haul furniture around northern Wyoming when you factored in tips.

New Barrett wanted to act out this particular fantasy with Chastity instead. He could imagine her in a tiny, pleated skirt that covered almost nothing. Cotton panties. Pierced nipples trying to rip through the thin fabric of her tight white uniform top. Rainbow pigtails perfectly angled for makeshift handlebars. Cheap red sucker rolling against her tongue...

The slight lines around Mrs. Walton's mouth struggled to twist upward into a Botox-deadened smile.

"My grades are slacking."

She sashayed up to him in her own uniform short skirt, hand stroking his bare pec beneath the open neckline of his button-down.

"I'm in desperate need of some one-on-one tutoring."

He chuckled, pulling her hand away from his chest. "Under different circumstances, this would be my lucky day, but sadly, this isn't that kind of business."

"Oh, come on. I paid for three hours of *deep* cleaning." Mrs. Walton leaned forward, squeezing her tits together, giving him a generous flash of bra-less -- impeccable -- implants through the low neckline of her schoolgirl's shirt.

His usual urge to fight an erection wasn't there. Something sexy was happening, but his hard-on was nowhere to be found. It was certainly curious.

Before he could give it any more thought, she gestured to a plush leather couch next to a brown-and-white cowhide rug. "I won't tell if you won't, Professor."

This was it. Fourteen-year-old Barrett's dream.

Getting *paid* to fuck.

As the urge to leave strengthened, the pimple-faced teenager from his past beat against the inside of his skull, screaming, 'Don't be a fool!"

Walton was beautiful. *Willing*. She craved what he had to offer: No strings attached cock.

"I assure you," she sat down on the couch, knees ever-so-slightly parting in his direction, "your tip will be more than generous."

The immature Barrett wanted to make a joke about *his* tip, a pun that would make her laugh until those silicone D-cups actually jiggled.

But he held back. He wondered for a moment if this was a test from Will and Ava? A set-up. A sting operation to see if he would stay true to his word about not risking the reputation of their business to a prostitution scandal.

From the couch, her sapphire eyes combed over every inch of him with an appreciative gaze.

"If you're having difficulties, I can promise that my grades won't be the *only* thing I can get up with a little hard work and guidance."

She winked. Her strawberry-colored lips were glossed, a thin sheen over a half-cocked grin.

"Can I ask you something?"

"*Mmmmmm*," she moaned.

"Why the Professor outfit?" He was eager to change the subject, waltzing back over to her windows to study the unbelievable view.

Mrs. Walton sighed at the momentary setback and leaned back into the couch. "I lost my virginity to my Women's Studies teacher at UW at the time."

Barrett smiled. *There was always a reason.* Somehow, Will had learned how to tap into those deeper desires of the women in Jackson and had curated an eclectic but effective arsenal of choices on the website's drop-down menu.

"There is something so hot about a man in charge when you're young and naive. We fucked like bunnies the entire semester." She sighed. "I think about him all the time."

Barrett turned in time to see the woman slowly popping the buttons of her shirt open. He cleared his throat.

"I'm afraid I really can't."

"Is it because I'm a student?" She grinned in character. "I promise, Professor, your wife will never find out. And I would never do anything to jeopardize your tenure at the school…"

"No," Barrett said, wincing. "I'm not playing the role, Mrs. Walton. I'm telling you that I really *can't*. No sex with the clients. It's one of our cardinal rules at *Man Maid*, unfortunately. So that makes this," he said, gesturing between them, "a no-fly zone. I'm so sorry."

With a sigh, her shoulders slumped. "Well, this is embarrassing." Her eyes filled with tears, and she turned away. "God, I'm so pathetic."

"No! Not at all." He waved away her words in the air. "You're gorgeous and adventurous. If this were any other situation, we'd be *destroying* that fucking cowhide rug right now. But I really like this job. I get to meet people like you and see places like this." He motioned around him. "I don't want to jeopardize that."

His mind flashed to Chastity.

Even though they weren't dating, he felt a small pang of guilt for even considering fucking the desperate housewife before him.

"Plus, I'm getting to know someone. I really like her. I'm tryin' real hard not to screw things up before anything can even get started."

"Pfft." She scoffed with sad eyes, her face looking ten years older as she frowned. Her tone grew nasty like a switch had flipped. "You think life is gonna be sunshine and roses now that you found someone special? Ugh. *Please*," she spat. "Wait until you're asking each other to check each other's moles and pissing with the bathroom door wide open. Relationships are *messy*. They're ugly and exhausting. When I said 'I do,' I thought we'd be together in the good times *and* the bad. But that workaholic asshole is never even *here*."

"Well, with all due respect, banging your maid probably isn't a step in the right direction for your marriage."

"What the hell would you know about *marriage*?" she snarled. Her eyes were hard, like those of a wounded animal. "You have *fuck boy* written all over you."

"You might be right," he said sternly. "I *don't* know a goddamned thing about marriage from experience. But before my parents died, I remember the way they looked at each other. I remember the way their voices softened when they talked to one another. Hell, even my grandparents… I remember my grandmother sitting by my grandfather's side for *weeks* in the hospital until the day the pneumonia finally took him. I see how lost she is without him every time I look into her eyes. To this *day,* she can't sleep a full night without him in bed beside her. She calls me at three in the morning sometimes just to hear a familiar voice. So, sure, I'm a '*fuck boy*' because that level of pain and *loss* scares the absolute *shit* out of me."

Barrett started to leave and then walked back again, standing in front of her on the cowhide rug, voice softer. "I see in you what I see in my grandmother: a lost woman who needs some companionship."

Those words hit her hard. She looked away.

"So, look all you want. Fill your spank bank with images of the ripped teacher in your den to use with your rabbit vibe the second I leave, but that's it. If you want to fire me… I can't stop you." He patted the sides of his slacks. "But next time… if there *is* a next time… if you want to use my body, use my *ears*. If you want to talk, I'm actually a way better listener than I am a mopper."

She laughed through tears. "I should hope so. You missed a *huge* chunk of the kitchen."

"*Fuuuuuck*," he groaned, deflated. "Sorry. I'll redo it. Although, in my defense, you have the biggest goddamn kitchen I've ever seen in my *life*."

She laughed and wiped a tear from her cheek. "It's fine. Get it next time."

"Yeah?" He sounded hopeful at the chance to return.

"I apologize. When Will used to come, he used to…" She blushed.

"Will used to *what*?" Barrett was genuinely curious now. "Fuck you?"

"No! He used to… *talk dirty*. Threatened to bend me over and spank my ass with a ruler if I misbehaved."

"Did he actually spank you?"

She shook her head. "Just the dirty talk."

Barrett thought for a moment.

Technically, a spanking didn't fall under the umbrella of prostitution, at least to his knowledge.

"You got a ruler? Like, a foot-long one?"

The question turned her on in an instant, eyes almost twinkling with arousal. She squirmed against the cushion of the couch unknowingly. "Yes. It's metal, and it makes one *hell* of a smack."

"Where is it?"

"It's in my office."

"*Get it*," Barrett ordered. "N*ow*."

She gasped and scurried into the back.

She wasn't firing him, which felt like a blessing. A couple of hard whacks against her silken-panty-clad cheeks from the mean ol' Professor's ruler would be a small price to pay to keep her as a happy, loyal client.

Hell, with how thirsty she'd seemed a few minutes earlier, Barrett knew it would probably make the broad's whole month.

26

A bright pink golf ball tumbled into the fifth hole of the tiny green with a dull *clink*.

"Fuck yeah!" Barrett shouted, pumping his fist in the air as Chastity stifled a laugh.

Suddenly, he remembered where they were and swallowed hard. He looked around. Two sets of parents, each with several young children, gawked at him. One family was ahead a few holes, the other behind. Both in earshot.

"Sorry!" he shouted, waving at both families apologetically. "I just... uh... got the ball in the thing."

One of the mothers shook her head.

"Smooooooooth," Chastity mocked.

Barrett shot her a glance and stepped off the green. "Says the *loser*."

"By *one* point! Hardly a margin to brag about."

The rustling wind tousled Chastity's loose curls, setting sun bathing her in a golden glow. Barrett found his brown eyes transfixed on her form as she readied herself on the green, small putter in hand. She bent down, eyed the hole, and shuffled her feet.

Her shoulders peeked out of a salmon-colored top with cutouts, shapely ass tucked into tight, complimentary shorts. Despite the chilly temperatures, she didn't wear a coat either, a common occurrence for many Wyomingites in the late spring.

His mind flashed to images of himself bending her backward over the hip-height windmill on the next hole, stripping her down, and burying his tongue between her bare thighs. His cock swelled against his denim. He adjusted himself discretely, shifting his weight, crossing his arms over his tight-fitting, heathered Henley shirt.

Chastity gently tapped the ball, watching as it tumbled into the hole.

"This was a par three. Got it in one. Guess who is trailing one point behind now?" she taunted smugly, shimmying her hips as she bent down to retrieve her gold ball.

She caught his eyes lingering and smiled, her cheeks turning a peachy pink as she blushed. "Whatcha lookin' at?"

"I'm looking at the next Tiger Woods. You should think about goin' pro."

"Oh." She leaned up toward his ear. He could feel her hot breath graze the outer shell, sending tingles down his neck and arms. "I thought you were just lookin' at my ass."

He chuckled, heading toward the next leg of the course. "Stop trying to distract me."

Once there, she shook her head. "Me? I am just *existing*."

"That's distraction enough." He set his pink golf ball back on the starting marker.

"Why fluorescent pink? Are you trying to prove how secure you are in your masculinity? Or do you just like the color?"

Barrett followed her eyes to his ball, furrowing his brow. "Actually, it's less of a fluorescent and more of a *flamingo* pink. Working at that picky-ass boutique, you, of *all* people, should know the subtle nuances of color. Imagine I ordered a flamingo pocket square, and you gave me *fluorescent* pink?"

"Fair enough."

He took a swing. His ball bounced off several wooden triangles, falling short of the hole and rolling backward off a sloped platform.

"To answer the question, I just like the color. Women don't own pink, and men don't own blue."

Barrett tapped the ball twice more, finally landing it into the hole.

Chastity placed her ball on the starting mark and wiggled her ass again.

"Would you stop that? These poor kids don't need to see me get a hard-on."

Chastity laughed. "What? I'm just getting into position." She wiggled her butt again.

"You're a *monster*." Barrett groaned.

Despite the comment's intention being flirtatious, Chastity felt a pang of hurt, as if there was some truth to it. As if he somehow saw through her and saw the same thing she saw in herself, like she had some hideous beast dormant beneath her skin. Even though she knew he didn't mean it like that, his words felt like they confirmed her worst fears.

Thrown off-kilter, she whacked her ball, giving the ball too much juice and bouncing it off the wooden guides back onto the course they had just finished with.

"Whoa." He seemed stunned by her sudden loss of skill. "I'll get it." As he brushed past her, he muttered, "No more bending over for *you*."

After he retrieved the gold ball, he bent over to put it in front of her, wiggling his own butt, coaxing an involuntary laugh from her. The simple act was enough to draw her out of her suffocating thoughts and back into the moment.

"Hmmm. I see what you mean about it being distracting." She cupped one of his jean-covered cheeks and, after a squeeze, pushed him out of her way.

As she tapped the ball again, softer this time, Barrett spoke. "When you're not on the GPA tour circuit, what sort of trouble do you get up to?"

"Well," she eyed the course, trying to calculate the best angle, "As you may have noticed at Nussbaum's house, I'm a bit of a reality television connoisseur."

"Well," Barrett jokingly tossed his putter into the real shrubs nearby and started to walk away, "thanks for the date. This was fun. Buh-bye."

"Why does everyone say that? They wouldn't have so many reality shows if people didn't watch them. They're so fun!"

"Watching angsty housewives slap each other around is not my idea of entertaining."

"Oh, stop. They're not all like that. I know a few *you* might even like."

Chastity tapped the ball. It approached the hole and whirled around the plastic outer edge without going in. She cursed under her breath.

"I highly doubt that." He scribbled their scores on the notepad as she gave the ball the two-inch tap it needed to go in.

"*Finally.*"

"Okay, besides your terrible taste in television, what else do you like?"

"I love animals. I volunteer at the shelter a lot. There's this Mastiff up there, Molly, that I'm in *love* with. I wish I could adopt her."

"Why can't you?"

"Money. Plus, I don't think *Rabbit Run* allows pets. Although, the people living in that apartment before me were clearly living *like* animals."

"No kidding. That place was a fuckin' zoo." Barrett laughed. "Animals, huh? I can get behind dogs, but what about other things? Like, you aren't into snakes and tarantulas and stuff, are you?"

He hit the ball just enough to roll it in. When he looked up, he noticed Chastity with her head cocked to the side like a German Shepard.

"What's wrong with snakes and tarantulas?"

"C'mon, really? They're snakes and spiders. People's two most common phobias. What good are they other than to scare the crap outta people?"

"Snakes keep pests under control. They help prevent the spread of diseases like Lyme, Lepto, and Hantavirus. Spiders do the same thing. They're also good for soil aeration and, like bees, most don't harm humans unless they feel threatened."

Barrett blinked repeatedly, unsure if he was dreaming. "So, you are saying you like *every* animal."

"Not all." She smiled. "Can't stand Pomeranians. They're like feather dusters that bite." She giggled. "I love all types of animals. Wouldn't want them all as *pets*, but everything has an important part to play in this world."

"So, are you gonna freak out if I squash a spider?"

"No." She laughed. "I get it. They're freaky, and most people don't know the good ones from the dangerous ones. I'm just saying I like everything because it all... *belongs*. It all has a purpose."

The father of the family behind them cleared his throat, impatiently waiting for his family's turn. He gave them a flat smile and squinted his eyes uncomfortably. "Can we play through?"

"Sure! Sorry," Chastity said.

They stepped aside, allowing the two small children to squabble over who would go first. The man stared at Chastity for a moment too long, and Barrett flashed him a sharp "F*uck off*" glare before draping his muscular arm over her bare shoulders.

The man turned around just in time to watch his son swing and miss the ball.

Chastity leaned up toward Barrett's ear. "Pfft, look at these amateurs. This guy with the beer gut and the two boys, he's definitely got a tattoo he regrets, like a half-sleeve portrait of Pee-Wee Herman on his bicep or something."

"You think so?" he murmured into her ear.

"I told you. I have a sixth sense about these things." She shrugged. "But, I guess even Paul Reubens is better than a *boo-bee.*"

"*Hey now,*" he playfully warned.

"You were perfect for *Man Maid.* Even your *tattoos* wear costumes."

"I'm feeling some real judgment about my ink right now."

She snickered, and then her eyes met his. Barrett wanted to lean down and kiss her. For a moment, the world around them seemed to fade away.

"There are corruptible kids around, or I'd be kissing the hell out of you right now," he mumbled against the side of her forehead.

"Same."

She turned back toward the course as the second child finally swatted his ball into the hole.

"Thanks," the man with the dad-bod said with a wave.

Barrett nodded and set his ball on the green.

"What about you?" Chastity asked.

"Ask me anything."

"With *this*… with *us*… are you looking for, you know, like, just a hook-up or… something *more*? I just wanna temper my expectations here."

Thrown off by the question, Barrett hit the ball too hard. It bounced out of the boundary and whacked the children's father in the ankle. The man whipped around and picked it up.

"Sorry!" Barrett croaked with an apologetic face, rushing over to retrieve the pink ball. "My bad."

Chastity covered her mouth to hide her smile and pointed at Barrett. "Penalty stroke!"

Barrett waltzed back with wide eyes and put the ball back at the starting mark.

Finally, when she stopped laughing, she said, "So, tell me what *you* enjoy."

He swung his putter again, driving his ball to the other side of the green and watching it roll lazily down into another sloped pit. "Well, at the moment, *not-effing-putt-putt*."

"Nah, I picture you as more of a full-contact sports guy."

"Nailed it. Football. It's a thing of beauty sometimes, seeing drafted nobodies become all-time legends who want to turn each other into drooling quadriplegics. Now *that's* a real man's game. Beyond that, I love shaking my ass at the country bars. I enjoy working out and getting a good sweat going. Obviously, I prefer *some* forms of exercise over others." He turned his head toward Chastity and flashed a knowing grin.

"Favorite team?"

"Wyoming Cowboys, obviously for college. Probably the Bills for the NFL."

"Wow, even into college ball, eh?"

"Of *course*." He tapped the ball in, scribbled on his scorecard, and gestured that it was her turn.

"Not bad." She frowned, swinging her putter in a circle.

"I believe what you meant to say was, Barrett, your skill is astounding. You're the master of mini-golf. Take me right here on the green and put your ball in my hole, you big stud-muffin."

"Ewwwww." Chastity snickered. "I would never call a grown man a 'stud-muffin.' Not even if I hated him."

She tapped her gold ball with startling precision. Another hole-in-one. She gloated, and they moved on.

"Last hole. You go first this time." Barrett tossed her the dimpled ball and pressed himself against her back. Her body tensed, subtly pressing back against him, feeling the heat from his body warm her own.

He spoke into her ear, voice gravelly, dripping with sensuality. "You might be schooling me out here on the course, but back in the bedroom, I think I could still teach you a thing or two about proper putter handling."

"Oh yeah?" She swung too hard again and accidentally whacked the ball out of the course boundary, this time smacking the meaty back of the same father's thigh as he stood at the club return window.

"Ow!" The man hissed, turning, glaring at them with a look of simmering rage.

"Holy crap!" She jogged over to retrieve it. "Sir, I am so sorry. This thing has a mind of its own. I swear, I wasn't aiming for you."

"Be careful!" he growled, slamming the ball back into her palm. "I'm gonna have a *bruise* now!"

"Won't happen again."

She walked back to Barrett, making a face of pure embarrassment. "Fuck, that was mortifying."

"I don't know whether to penalize you a point or *gift* you one. That was impressive."

Chastity looked at the final course. "How about this. *I* know I beat you. *You* know I beat you. How about we play this one for all the marbles? The loser buys the winner a round at *The Alibi*."

Barrett held his hand out, and she shook it.

"Girl, brace yourself. Get that wallet ready. I feel like some *top-shelf* liquor tonight!"

27

"Sixty-eight dollars for four drinks? Girl, that was half my damn tip yesterday!" Barrett laughed. "You are so not a cheap date!"

"Hey, I didn't make the rules."

"Yes, you did!" he exclaimed playfully.

Barrett's Jeep was backed up a few feet away from the treacherous edge of a mountain in the small dirt parking lot of one of the many scenic lookouts in the Grand Tetons. The spot provided a breathtaking view of Jackson, the city small and glinting in the low groove between the mountain ranges. Beams of light stroked the homes there with ethereal fingertips. Green expanses of untouched land spread out around the edges for miles, dotted with elk and cars along the thoroughfare, cutting through the edge of it all.

With the trunk door open wide, Barrett and Chastity sat in the back, bundled together in a fleece blanket, watching in serene silence as the sun lowered toward the horizon, bathing everything in a soft, daffodil-colored glow.

As the minutes ticked on, streetlights ignited, glittering like fireflies in the distance. Leaning back, Chastity breathlessly gazed at dusk's palette of plums and tangerines along the scattered clouds that had formed far overhead. Tears pricked her eyes as she appreciated the view, so glad to be in this moment with a man beside her who made her heart and stomach dance.

Barrett leaned against the backing of the rear seats, ignoring a view that would still the heart of the finest painter, instead focused on the glint of tears in Chastity's ochre eyes.

"Why are you crying?" he asked gently, with no hint of judgment or humor in his tone.

"Oh," she said, allowing the tears to fall from her face.

Barrett watched as the stream of liquid captured the colors of the evening sky as it traveled to her quivering lips.

"I can't seem to control it. Just… my fucked-up emotions getting the best of me. Being bipolar sucks, sometimes."

Barrett wiped her cheek softly. "Don't do that."

"Do what?"

"Chalk having emotions up to some disorder. You're not expected to be a robot.

Emotions make us human. You're allowed to *feel*."

Chastity clamped her hands together nervously. "I guess I didn't realize I was doing that."

They sat in silence, one eventually broken by a sharp sniffle. "When you find out you have this... *thing*... inside of you that's wrong, you question every emotion, every feeling, wondering if it's normal, you know?"

"I can't name one single normal person. Normal isn't real. It doesn't exist. Chastity, you are *extraordinary*. You... *who* you are... everything *you* are, is completely one-of-a-kind."

Chastity shifted herself up to the edge of the trunk, wiggling her feet restlessly above the dirt.

After a moment, Barrett spoke again. "Ever since you told me about the diagnosis, I've been thinking a lot about it. About *you*. And about my high school friend. I wondered for a *long* time if I could've done or said something to save him. I tried to put myself in Alan's shoes to understand why he thought it was the right decision to leave this world, and I just... couldn't. I watched him wither up, mentally, afraid to seek any help, afraid to take any meds. He let it define him."

Barrett sighed long and deep.

"He didn't *have* the disorder. It had *him*."

Chastity's voice was small. "I'm sorry… about your friend."

"It honestly broke my heart. He started isolating himself and self-medicating with drugs. One night, he just… took too much. Wanted to take it all away, I suppose. Wanted to stop it all. The good *and* the bad."

Chastity's tears suddenly emerged again. "You know it wasn't your job to save him, right? You couldn't control how he handled it."

"I know." He shifted forward, lifting her colorful hair and kissing the back of her neck. In between kisses, he spoke. "I just don't ever want to see you go down the same path."

She nodded.

"I shouldn't be giving you life advice, though. I'm a fucking mess myself."

She snickered through the tears. He slid his legs around her and massaged her shoulders. She moaned, leaning back into his body.

"I'm a grown-ass man who wears Halloween costumes for a living. I don't know what I'm doing. I have no idea where I am going or what I want, except for *this*… right now."

He stared past her at the sun as it nestled behind the steep mountains. "I live in a pig sty, and I get into dumb bar fights. I'm just a fuckin' mess."

Barrett reached behind him and unzipped an insulated bag, pulling a plastic-wrapped sub out and placing it in her hands.

"Awww, you made me a sandwich?" she asked.

He laughed. "*Hell no.* I'm a terrible cook, too. I like you too much to put you through that. This is from the deli by my place. Best sandwiches in Jackson. I got you what I normally order. Hope that's alright."

Grasping the delicately wrapped sandwich, she nodded, offering him a broad smile. "Thank you."

Chastity took a bite and was pleasantly surprised at the delicate, airy ciabatta bread encasing fresh veggies, turkey, provolone, and a white sauce she couldn't place.

"Damn, that's good. What the hell is this sauce? I want a *gallon* of it."

"It's good, right?"

She nodded with her mouth full. Once she swallowed, she spoke. "I'm a damned mess, too. I loathe dishes. I'm always dying my hair. I need a lot of attention, as terrible as that sounds. I don't vote. I smoke weed sometimes to help me sleep when I'm amped up. I cry, obviously. Sometimes, a lot. Sometimes, for seemingly no reason, have since I was a kid."

"I like you." He twisted a finger around one of her loose curls and nuzzled the shell of her ear with his nose. "Tears and all."

He kissed her neck again, lips and tongue stroking the delicate skin there. He breathed her in. "I can still smell just the faintest hint of your jasmine perfume on my pillow."

"Eww," she joked quietly, "you never *washed* it?"

"The rest of the bedding, yes. The pillow, no. It's all I had left of you."

He gently stroked the bare flesh of her shoulder with his thumb. "I think about that night all the time."

Chastity cleared her throat, her voice coming out more hushed than before. "I do, too."

Hope effervesced deep in his chest, making him feel impossibly light. She was like a missing piece of the puzzle within him, a feeling that struck him with equal parts joy and terror.

"I keep having dreams that I'm in the rainforest, hopelessly lost, and all of a sudden, I peel back these leaves, looking for a path, and I see it there… this bright, blue orchid, growing out from between the cracks of a rock wall. This beautiful thing is just there… thriving, rooted in such an inhospitable place. And then I wake up, and I realize it's your tattoo. But more than that, it's *you*, this rare and delicate thing, splitting rock, laughing in the face of adversity."

Chastity couldn't find the words to reply.

"I meant to ask… why a blue orchid?" His hand slid beneath the hem of her shirt, stroking the sensitive skin where her inked image resided.

"They represent rarity and calmness. Seeing it reminds me to focus when my emotions are getting the best of me."

"I like that."

With his hand beneath her shirt, he tickled her for a moment. She giggled joyfully and nearly dropped the last bit of her sandwich.

"Stop," she begged.

Barrett's fingers slowed. He closed his eyes and wished he could capture the sound of her laughter to play on repeat forever.

Chastity finished her sandwich, hopped out, and walked to the edge of the lookout, peering down at the height of the drop-off and staring out at the dusky sky. "It's stunning out here."

"You've never been?" Barrett scooted to the edge of the Wrangler, allowing his cowboy boots to drag in the dirt.

"No, not to this lookout." Chastity returned to him, leaning in for a kiss, lips soft and warm.

He wrapped his arms around her. As the kiss deepened, she climbed atop his lap. His eyes widened with surprise as she nestled onto him.

His hands ran up her bare thighs, his erection emerging between them, stiff and hard beneath his zipper.

He pulled his face away, eyes peering into hers as if to assure that she was alright, searching her flushed face for any sign of unease. When he saw nothing, he gestured to his crotch. "Sorry about him. Poor bastard has no manners."

Instead of a verbal reply, she ground her needy pelvis against his lap, diving back in to claim his mouth with her own. As their lips met, the current between them grew to the force of a riptide, and he purred. His demanding hands gripped her, winding around slowly into her shorts to massage her ass.

His stubble scraped against her chin. Her hair tickled the sides of his face. Their breathing turned ragged as they squirmed, one of his hands moving to the back of her neck to pull her closer.

She pulled away for a moment, eyes lusty, even in the waning light.

"What's wrong?" he panted.

She looked around. "Now that the sun's down, it's freezing out here."

"Want to move this party to the back seat?"

She nodded, and a mischievous smile spread all the way across her face. She hopped out again and crawled into the back seat. Barrett closed up the hatch, turned on the car, and cranked the heater.

"Ummm, Barrett?"

"Yeah?" As soon as he looked in the back, he let out an exasperated sigh. "Dammit, you weren't supposed to see that yet. I was going to give that to you at the end of the night."

"This is for me?!" she shouted.

"You don't know how hard it was for me to find a blue orchid around these parts."

"Barrett!" She clutched the pot of the sickly, spindly plant to her chest.

"It needs a bit of TLC."

She fingered the pale cerulean petals and gave him a smile of appreciation. "Thank you. I love it."

"Happy housewarming."

She squealed, handing it up to him. "Would you put it on the floorboard? I don't want her getting crushed."

"Sure thing."

He set the planter on the floor and joined her in the back seat. They stared at each other for a moment, Chastity's smile fading back into something more intense. Her breath hitched as he approached, running his fingers through the hair at the base of her neck, gripping some with a firm and steady fist. He licked his lips, eyes refocusing on her mouth, pulse thundering in his neck like a jackhammer.

Her head drifted back with the pressure of his grasp, and she let out a soft moan as he caressed the exposed skin of her neck and shoulders with his mouth. She squeezed her legs together to ease the ache as his tongue glided across her chest, plunging down into the top of her bra as he pulled her hair back harder.

She was frozen in his grasp. Too eager to breathe right. To turned-on to think.

He kissed the flesh of her upper breast and latched on hard, sucking forcefully enough to leave a solid mark. He pulled away seconds later with a wet *pop*.

"Did you just give me a hickey?" She pulled away from his grip enough to look down. "Are we in *high school*?"

His lips curled into a grin, eyes full of something wild and enticing. "I wanted you to have something to remember me in the coming days. This should keep the boys at bay, so you have time to give it some thought. If you want to be with me, *I don't share.*"

Part of her wanted to be offended, but the act... the magenta mark it left... the ownership it displayed made her utterly turned on.

"I think I want *more*, Aphrodite."

"Of what?"

"Of *you*. I knew the second I laid eyes on you that you were intoxicating. If you don't feel the same, I understand. But tonight, I'm satisfied leaving you with a little reminder, a little sign to show the other men I call dibs."

She pulled her shirt down to see the small circle on her breast. "Dibs? I'm not a piece of meat or a plot of land to claim." Her voice raised a little and lowered again as he caressed her inner thigh. "What if I have no *clue* what I want?"

"Take a beat to decide, Aphrodite. We can fool around if that's all you want, but I'd like more. I want you to be *mine* and mine alone."

"And you'd be mine?"

"Yes."

"Mine... *and all the horny wives of Jackson.*"

"That's just a job, Chastity. I'm not fucking them. I'm talking about a relationship. I'm talking about coffee in the morning or stroking your hair while we fall asleep watching trash reality shows. I'm talking about a future and trust."

"Can't we just... I don't know..."

"Chastity, now that I've had you, I want *all* of you. If you don't want me, we can go back to playing the field. But I don't want to be half-in this thing, whatever it is. I want you. All of you. Body and soul. I won't settle for anything less."

Barrett shifted back into his seat until he was staring out of the windshield.

"Alright." She laughed and grabbed the seat belt behind her. "So you're just gonna drop me off all wound up with a purple hickey on my boob?"

Barrett chuckled. "Part of you is *purple*." He looked down at his lap. "Part of me is *blue*. I'd say we're just about even."

There was a long silence where only the wind spoke in a quiet howl, rocking the Jeep a little before dying down.

Finally, she spoke.

"Barrett, I really like you..."

"But...?"

"But... I don't want to drag you -- or *anyone* -- into my bipolar shit-storm. This... us... it's poor timing."

"I'm a big boy. I'm no stranger to a shit-storm. Give me a *chance*. Let me decide for myself what I can handle."

"I have no idea what I want out of life, Barrett."

"You're twenty-five. You don't *have* to have it all figured out yet." His eyes were fixed on hers. "Chastity, I fucking *want* you."

"I want you, too," she said softly. "I'm just... *scared*."

He pressed his forehead to hers, tenderly stroking her jaw.

Without another word, she bolted forward, pressing her lips to his and kissing him with urgency, hands clutching his hair, his shirt, his belt, needing him, needing to not lose him, needing to feel everything about him in and on her body all at once.

He fumbled with the button on her shorts. Her chest heaved as he tugged down her zipper, exposing the lacy black fabric obscuring the bald, sensitive skin beneath.

Kneeling up on the seat, he climbed across to her, his lips pressing against hers more gently this time, thumbs hooking her underwear, other fingers clenching, pulling down, prying all fabric off her ass like a magician trying to whip away a tablecloth while leaving the plates. She bucked her hips up to assist, helping him yank her clothes roughly down her thighs, stopping at her ankles.

His eyes lapped at every inch of silky smooth skin, narrowing with a look of barely-contained desire. He unzipped his pants, reached in, and fisted the bulge, giving himself a stroke outside the fabric of his briefs.

He tugged her shorts and panties around her untied shoes, tossing the wadded clothing onto the floorboard.

"*Spread your pretty little legs for me,*" he murmured with a groan. "*Show me how you want me to touch you. Show me how you like to be touched.*"

A heady mixture of lust and want washed through her, dampening everything between her legs as she propped a foot high up on the passenger seat headrest, the other trembling in the crevice of the back seat. She slid her hands down to her wet, aching pussy. As her fingers rounded her thigh, he watched intensely, like a man possessed. The sight of her fingertips swirling gently against her swollen clit made him feel light-headed.

"Fuck, baby. You look incredible," he gritted out, voice lowering an octave beneath the weight of his desire.

He'd give every dime he had to stop time itself, making this moment last as long as it possibly could.

Her fingers glistened beneath the dome light's beam. Barrett leaned through the seats and turned the radio dial slightly, changing the music to a song with a fitting tempo, one that pulsed like her strokes.

Chastity's chest heaved, her eyes locked on his as they roamed her body. Her mouth fell open as the tight bundle of nerves between her legs shot a bolt of ecstasy through her. Her back arched at the pleasure brought to her by her own hands.

Barrett's jealous mouth watched, parched like a man in the desert looking at the sweet, wet oasis that beckoned him.

A spot of pre-cum dampened the front of his pants, cowboy boots grinding noisily against the dirt and rocks beneath his feet. The cold night air nipped at his back while the heaters inside blasted.

His jaw tightened, greedy gaze locked on her shaking, parted legs. He scooped his arms under her knees and yanked her across the seat toward the open door.

She playfully yelped and giggled, and he dropped to his knees on the rough terrain. Barrett spread her thighs and dove in, lightly swiping his tongue up, savoring the taste of her. She gasped at the first contact and then relaxed, slowly tilting her hips up toward his mouth. He alternated between gentle sucks and languid strokes, stubble skimming her most intimate parts, sending goosebumps up her legs.

His moan vibrated against her, and soon, he felt her breath hitch and her muscles pulse. Her body glistened with a thin sheen of sweat.

Enjoying every second of his lavish laps, Chastity shut her eyes, fingers moving through his black hair and gripping the back of his neck.

The delicious sensation soon gave way to euphoria. Her entranced eyes pinched closed as another moan escaped her lips.

One of his hands snaked up the crease of her thigh, dipping beneath the hem of her blouse, pushing up her bra with his fingers before making contact with one of her piercings. Her back arched as he relentlessly rolled the studded pebble between his fingers.

Chastity groaned, pressing her clit against his mouth, chasing the high of another imminent orgasm.

Barrett pulled away and licked his glistening lips. "You're a greedy little thing. *I love it.*"

She whined, body writhing, seeking more contact. He slowly blew cool air against her hot folds, watching her body grow rigid and then relax again. When he resumed, the renewed heat of his tongue against her skin brought her right back to the cliff's edge, ready to plummet swiftly.

His lips and tongue pulled away, and his other hand made its way to her entrance. He inched two fingers inside of her, making her gasp.

"You like that?"

"*Mmmm-hmmmm,*" she purred, nodding at him.

"Whose pussy is this?" He slid his fingers out and back in again as slowly as he could possibly manage.

"*Hmmmm?*" He pressed in again, curling them up into her depths for pressure.

"*Say it*, Aphrodite."

He slipped his fingers in a third time.

"Whose... fucking... gorgeous," he sucked the juices off of her folds hard enough to pinken them instantly, "bare... little... pussy *is* this, Aphrodite?"

"*Yours,*" she finally whispered, laying her head back and moaning from another plunge of his slippery fingers. "*That's your pussy.*"

She shoved her hips down against him, sinking him deeper into her warmth.

"That's right. That's *mine.*" He slid his flattened tongue in circles around her clit again. "Is my beautiful little pussy gonna cum again for me?"

She moaned, clutching at the seat belt and bucking him again. He spread her thighs wider and dipped his tongue inside of her.

"*Fuck.*"

He pulled back and smiled, wearing her juices like chapstick. "*You...* like *this.* You're the only fucking meal I ever want to eat again."

His mouth consumed her with a new, fevered urgency.

"Oh, God," she croaked. "Barrett, you're... you're gonna make me cum."

Her muscles clenched around his fingers as she came again. Her back arched with wave after wave of intense pleasure.

Suddenly, they both froze as gravel crunched beneath tires in front of Barrett's Jeep. They panicked frantically, scrambling to find her pants on the floor.

"*Shit*," he hissed, looking back at the approaching squad car.

"Fuck." Chastity scrambled to pull her pants right-side-out, shoving her legs clumsily in the holes. Barrett shoved her feet inside, and the Jeep jostled as he shut the door. He stood in front of it, buying her a few more precious seconds to dress as the officer stepped out and approached on foot. He subtly zipped his jeans as the uniformed officer smiled.

It was John Ridgeway again.

"Fancy seeing you *twice* in one week, Barrett."

Barrett let out a laugh that was relief mixed with jumbled nerves. "What can I say? I missed you. Couldn't wait to hang out again."

"We gotta stop meeting like this," John laughed, shining his giant flashlight into the fogged back seat at Chastity. She waved, hair tangled, shirt hanging oddly.

"Don't either of y'all have a nice, warm, *private* bedroom?" John shined his light right into Barrett's eyes. After a second, he lowered it to Barrett's erection. "Happy to see me?"

Barrett covered the bulge with his hands.

"I'd say it's a little cold to be out here with no jacket, but it seems like you two are being creative at, uh, keeping things nice and *hot*."

Barrett smiled, embarrassed.

"You know, it's funny." John turned off his flashlight and clipped it on his cluttered utility belt. "I was just up here the other day busting some horny teenagers. This place is apparently called *Make-out Point* by the local kids who don't seem to *understand* that it's *illegal* to have sex in public. Wild, right?"

John had driven his point home.

"I know my jail is real cozy. But hows about you and her keep warm in a *hotel room* so I don't have to keep hauling your ass in? Hmm?"

"Sure thing." Barrett nodded.

"You two have a nice night." As Officer Ridgeway got back to his squad car, he spoke again. "Oh, and Barrett?"

"Yeah?"

He clicked on his flashlight again and shined it on the wad of lacy panties on the gravel near Barrett's boots. "Our motto out here is

'*Take only pictures, leave only footprints,*' ya hear?"

28

Maggie scanned the rows of cushioned chairs of the church for abandoned belongings and errant bibles, tidying up after her husband's congregation. She loved to care for God's temple with the reverence she knew it deserved.

Once everything had been picked up, she took a seat in the front row and glanced up at the ten-foot white cross on the wall as her thoughts drifted to her daughter. Chastity always had been a defiant child, emotional and difficult. Maggie remembered being beaten and punished for the same sort of outbursts when she was young, though it seemed her gentler style of parenting wasn't the answer either.

Where Maggie would've been grounded, Chastity had only gotten verbally reprimanded. Where Maggie was shaken or slapped, Chastity was only ever sent to her room. It had taken every ounce of her patience for her to deal with her daughter's antics as she became an adult, an adult who didn't seem to shy away from sin and tumbled into avoidable pitfalls constantly.

Maggie, on the other hand, had always fought to remain on the right path. Chaste and modest, never so much as letting a boy touch her breast until her wedding night. When she had her only daughter, she thought she had done the right thing involving her so heavily in her husband's ministry. She recalled the tantrums the child had frequently had out of boredom, ones that always left her in a pile of frilly lace and tears.

Maggie had grown up in the church, just as Chastity had. She recalled having the same sort of outbursts when she was a child. It was only when her beatings increased that she learned to numb herself, to disassociate from the feelings inside her, stuffing them down and locking them away where she could no longer feel them. She replaced them with an obsession to *do* right. To *act* right. To *be* right.

That lifestyle led Maggie on the path to Arnold and her daughter, to their beautiful home and a social status to be proud of.

Gone was the poor little child going to church with ratty shoes and second-hand dresses. She'd elevated herself to the kind of woman she would've looked up to as a child. Why her daughter refused to do the same, despite having every opportunity in life, completely baffled her.

Maybe Maggie *had* been too harsh lately. How many times had the Apostles spoken about forgiving sinners? The Bible said, '*Seventy times seven.*' While she surely exceeded those numbers for her daughter, if God could love a prostitute, a drunkard, and the dead, she could surely find a path back to loving her own flesh and blood.

"Maggie," a female's voice hollered behind her.

Spinning in the chair, she saw Sue Thompson. The bleach blonde seemed like the perfect embodiment of desecrating God's temple with implants, injections, tucks, and extensions. Nevertheless, Sue tithed consistently and seemed to show a real interest during their sermons, even volunteering to help with an event here and there.

"You're still here?" Maggie plastered on her most genuine smile, a fake expression she'd perfected over the years.

"Yeah, I was looking for my house key. I took it off my ring the other day to give to my housecleaning staff, and I think the darned thing fell out of my bag during today's service."

Maggie fished the key out of the pocket of her beige blazer and smiled. "It wouldn't be a Sunday service if someone didn't leave something behind."

"Oh, thank God!" Sue slapped her chest dramatically, but her boobs didn't move. "I thought I was gonna have to go back to Starbucks, too. Glad I stopped here first."

Maggie handed it back. "How have you been?"

"Great," Sue said, overenthusiastic as usual. She held up the key. "You know… funniest thing about this new cleaning service…"

"Do tell."

"Well, Barrett, you know that handsome man who came over during Bible study? Well, he actually works there."

"Oh, well, that makes sense."

"Well," Sue laughed and sat down in the next row, two feet from Maggie's chair, "he actually worked there before you all gave him all those tips. Remember how he said he ruined some towels? Those were mine." Her laughter resonated through the cavernous building. "He exploded my bath mat, too."

"Oh, you're kidding." Maggie tried to hide a big smile.

"No. And between you, me, and that podium, he does it almost in the *buff*."

"What?" Maggie's smile disappeared.

"Yeah, they're like… sort of like *Chippendales*. You know *Chippendales*?"

"Oh, yes, Chastity used to love those cartoons."

Sue barked a laugh. "No, not *Chip 'n Dale*. The male exotic dancers, silly. These men at *Man Maid*, they come and clean your house while they're in sexy little costumes, sometimes wearing practically nothing."

Maggie literally clutched her pearls, eyes drifting to the cross on the wall and back to Sue.

She suddenly remembered the stinging words of her daughter's impromptu bible lesson. "Oh. Well, how he earns his money is hardly my business."

"Well, I suppose it's at least a little bit your business if he might end up being your son-in-law one day."

Maggie was confused. "What are you talking about?"

"Well, him and Chastity, of course."

Maggie still looked confused.

"Oh, don't tell me in a town this small you haven't heard."

"Him and Chastity?" The revelation made her feel dizzy.

"Yeah! My dog sitter said they were out there playing putt-putt down off 191. He said Barrett had his arm around her neck, whisperin' things in her ear, being all flirtatious and what-not." She burst into another loud laugh. "He... said... Chastity and him kept whacking him... in the leg... with the ball."

"You don't say." Maggie fought hard against the urge to grind her molars.

Sue howled louder, tears forming in her eyes. Any harder, and she was going to pee herself. "He... he showed me the bruises!"

29

"Alright. Let me see the goods." Maya clapped from the couch in her pink pinstripe blouse and gray slacks. Her black hair was clipped up, though her features seemed less youthful and vibrant than before.

Barrett happily obliged without a hint of hesitancy, posing confidently in her living room in a Roman-style toga draped over his shoulder, across his chest, and down to his shins. The ensemble was cinched at the waist with a decorative golden curtain tie, one that resembled a rope.

"So?" He stepped forward, sunlight glinting off a pair of gold sandals and a metal laurel leaf headband that pinned his raven-black hair against his temples. "What do you think?"

"The Romans would be appalled, but I love it."

"What? Why?"

"Well, for starters, the rich wore the longer togas like that. They could afford the extra fabric. It was a sign of opulence. Second, they were made of wool, not cheap polyester. They were also pinned, not sewn together, and they were a sign of status, so… having you wear a long toga to clean my house would have been fairly offensive."

Barrett laughed. "Hey, *Man Maid* never claimed to be historically accurate, just fun." He flexed his biceps. "I *dare* a Roman to make this outfit look this good."

"The empire fell in 476 A.D., so none could really contest you." Maya's features softened.

The bags under Maya's eyes were noticeable, and she didn't hold her smile long.

He tilted his head, looking her up and down. "You alright? You seem exhausted."

"Yeah, I'm fine. It's just… problems at work."

"Tell me about it."

She paused, spinning around. "I mean this with no offense, I swear, but… I don't think you'd understand it."

"So? I'm a good listener. Sometimes, talking it out helps." He took her by the hand and dragged her toward the kitchen. "I can listen while I clean."

"Dear God, where have men like you been my entire life?"

***

Two hours later, Barrett was still nodding along, listening intently as Maya wove a complicated tapestry of employee relationships and software jargon. She rambled on about software written in C++, which was, ironically, just about the grade he earned in his high school computer class.

She discussed the intricacies of code complications and how one small error somewhere could disrupt an entire software program. She'd been reviewing this particular section of code for three days and was unable to find the problematic issue.

"And now everything is starting to look like a blur. I have to fix this, but it's like my brain is completely fried. I am having trouble doing basic stuff like... deciding what to make for dinner and what shirt to wear for work. I'm somewhere between *frazzled* and needing a *shrink*."

"Can I ask you a question?"

"Sure." She nodded, reaching for the red wine decanter on the counter. Barrett tossed down his scrub sponge, wiped his hands on his toga, and took a seat beside her.

He watched as she poured herself another liberal glass of wine and held the rest of the bottle out to him. "Can I get you a glass?"

"No, thanks." He studied her face up close. "No offense, but Maya, when was the last time you slept?"

"Last night."

"For how *long*?"

She hesitated, swirling the liquid around her glass, eyes intensely focused on it to avoid eye contact.

"Three hours, give or take." She paused. "I *really* have to find this error. People are depending on me to find this one tiny little screw-up. Our clients are going to jump ship if I can't get it figured out, like *now*."

"Alright." He removed his golden headband and set it on her head. "Follow-up question… when was the last time you cut loose and did something other than this?"

She tried to think through the foggy haze of exhaustion and the hum of the wine.

"I'm not sure if you *heard me* when I said people need me to fix this. Our *company* is at stake. People's *jobs* are at stake. I can't just go off and have fun. That wouldn't solve anything."

"Maya, you deserve a life of your own. Your coding issue has had everything frozen for days, right?"

Nodding her head, tears welled in her tired eyes. She quickly wiped them away. "Yeah."

"One more night won't hurt."

She scoffed, shaking her head before Barrett gently grabbed her chin. "You have to clear your head. You are too close to the problem. You just gotta step away for a bit. Get some sleep. Get out and live a little."

"And do what? I don't have any friends here yet." She waved her glass, spilling a little bit of wine on the counter. Like lightning, Barrett was on his feet, snatching up a paper towel to clean it.

"What about your coworkers?" he asked sincerely, worried eyes staring at her with sincere concern. "Don't you have any work friends you can go get a bite to eat with? Or a beer?"

"Barrett, nobody wants to hang out with their boss in their free time."

"Come out with me tonight."

"Barrett, you are so out of my league it's uncomfortable to even look at you sometimes. I can't—"

"No, Maya, not on a *date*," he interrupted. "I'll introduce you to a few people here, one of which I think you might have stuff in common with. We'll drink, cut loose, and have a few beers. Hell, maybe break some laws. It'll be so fun. You gotta see some of Jackson Hole."

"I can't."

"Maya, let me show you a good time. We gotta get you out of this house. Please? For me?"

She pinched her eyes closed, shaking her head at his insistence. "Fine."

"Great. I'll swing by and pick you up at seven, alright?"

"You don't have to—"

"I know, but I want to. Until then, you have one assignment. And, Maya, this is crucial."

She stared up at him blankly.

"Take a *nap*. If anyone has earned it, it's you."

30

Chastity lurched up from the tufted lounger and paced the room. "You've got to be kidding me." She spat, more to herself than him. "This is *bullshit*."

"Sorry to say, but it isn't B.S., it's reality. I know you only came to me to get a second opinion, but I'm afraid I have to agree with your last therapist." His voice was even, almost disinterested.

"Not *my* reality!" she snapped. The anger inside of her was so tempestuous she feared she might set him aflame with the intensity of her stare. But a moment later, her snarl soon faded away to a hopeless regret. She knew she was feeding into the diagnosis, the stigma, but she couldn't seem to control her emotions. They always seemed to have a mind of their own. This moment was no exception.

Dr. Brown, contrary to his name, was a balding white man, though his clean-shaven face made him look younger than the age his crown of gray hair suggested he was. His hands rested in his lap near his bulging waistline, the button of his coat tilting up as the material stretched. His leather swivel chair creaked as he twisted this way and that in an attempt to follow her.

"So, that's it, then? I'm for sure bipolar? So now, I get to slap a warning label on my forehead for the rest of my life?"

"Based on what you've told me, you have had this for a long time. You have a *name* for it now. And that name comes with a world of options. You can start planning an attack, combating the extremes, leveling out your impulsivity, and so forth."

Chastity's eyes angrily roamed his office, one decorated with emotion-inducing paintings and several confidence-inspiring plaques, diplomas, and awards hung on the wall with care.

"How do you know for sure? You spent, what, an hour and fifteen minutes talking to me, and you just... *know*?"

He watched her pace. "You sent over your records from the college counselor. I reviewed them carefully. I've listened to you talk about your emotions, your mood swings, your impulsive behaviors. It's not a guess. I didn't get all those diplomas out of a Cracker Jack box. My DSM-V isn't just a bulky paperweight. I've been doing this almost longer than you've been alive."

She plopped back down on the chaise, collapsing into herself, the stubbornness of her denial the only thing keeping her upright.

"So.. now what?" A rush of emotion overtook her. Unable to hold them back, tears fell and spattered against the thighs of her torn jeans. "What do I do now?"

Dr. Brown leaned forward in his chair, his hazel eyes softening with some genuine compassion. "You have two options: you can continue to suffer manic highs and depressive lows, or… we can finally try something different. The choice is up to you."

"I just don't get it. I'm not some explosive person who has to be medicated to oblivion just so I can be more palatable to other people. I'm not that bad."

"It's not about making you socially palatable. It's less about your propensity for angry or tearful outbursts, more about how you *feel*."

"I feel fine," she lied.

"How have you been sleeping?"

"Fine," she said so weakly he almost couldn't hear her.

He tilted his head, giving her a discerning look. "I cannot help you if you aren't honest with me. The only person you're hurting here is yourself."

She sniffled. "You want honesty? Fine. I haven't slept more than three or four hours at a time in well over a month."

"And how has your mood been?"

"It's been good. I'm staying upbeat, considering the circumstances."

"Spending a lot of money?" he asked with a cocked eyebrow.

She laughed. "I don't have much to spend. I barely had enough to cover this visit."

"You do any gambling, street-racing, sex with strangers, self-harm?"

She waited a while, then finally nodded. "Yeah. Sex."

"All of them?"

"No, the sex. Some... one-night stands."

His expression never changed, as if he was expecting that answer. "Anything else? Substance abuse?"

"Occasional alcohol. A little weed."

"What about abrupt changes?"

"Like what?"

"Like, say, dying your hair all the colors of the rainbow?" He offered a small, knowing grin.

She twisted a strand of hair around her finger and laughed. He had her dead-to-rights. "Mayyyybe."

His grin grew into a humored smile as he swiveled back to his computer, the screen illuminating his face with a cold, blueish hue.

"That would be the mania. Right now, you might even feel like you're invincible. Bulletproof. Maybe you think that rules don't apply to you or that you have your life perfectly under control. Depending on where you are at, in a month or two, maybe longer, a low will come."

A pit opened in her stomach, and she suddenly felt drained of all color. It felt familiar, like something that routinely came and passed.

"Level with me, Ms. Erikson. How bad do the depressive episodes usually get? Do you swing in the opposite direction and sleep like it's a full-time job? Do you have very little motivation or difficulty keeping up with hygiene and showers?"

She nodded.

"Maybe you considered harming yourself?"

She thought back to the last time she felt down in the dumps. She'd been sleeping fourteen hours a day and considered the world might be a better place without her in it. She wondered if her friends and family might be relieved to no longer have her dragging them down with her.

A thought popped into her mind, flicking a switch in her that raised a brick wall of denial.

"I'm sorry. Dr. Brown, I know you think you know this kind of stuff, but I think you've misjudged me. I can hold down a job. I won awards in high school. For a while, I was acing my college classes. A sick person can't be *that* productive."

"There's a cycle of this disorder called *overachieving* that might sound familiar. You're productive, getting so much done that you continue piling more and more things on your plate. Then, because of the load, you start to fail, dropping those things *and* the plates. Then, that usually starts a cycle of depression because you can't seem to do all the million things you were doing a month ago. Then, you stop being productive altogether, feeling hopeless or useless until you slowly build yourself up again, gathering steam until the manic cycle starts up again." He looked over his shoulder at her. "Sound familiar?"

She winced as the pattern struck her like a blow to the temple, making her feel dazed as she reflected on her last few years in college and high school, both a blur of productivity followed by over-commitments to after-school clubs and advanced placement classes.

After a while, she would find herself skipping after-school meetings and struggling to turn assignments in on time.

"Maybe," she finally said. "But I don't flip out at *everything*. I'm not *violent*. I don't just snap."

"I don't know where you got this notion that bipolar means you're some kind of aggressive, raging beast. Bipolar people can be some of the nicest people you've ever met. Many of my favorite patients are bipolar. A mood disorder doesn't make you a monster."

She dug her nails into her palms in an attempt to distract her from the lump in her throat. Angry tears threatened to fall. She fought desperately to contain them, not wishing to seem any more the caricature of the disorder than she already felt she was.

"Now, if you want to treat this and get a handle on it, first, we need to set you up with regular appointments, either with myself or a counselor, so that we can assess your progress and help you monitor your moods. Cut out the alcohol and the weed. You don't need that stuff. They're masks for a problem, not fixes. We need to get you on a healthy diet... and sleep," he darted his eyes over to her, "sleep is *very* important."

"As far as medications, I will write you a script for an anti-psychotic that works well for this sort of thing. We can also start you on an antidepressant to help bring up those lows. There are quite a few with minimal side effects. Then, we can also try a mood stabilizer. One I like to start with is Lamotra—"

"Whoa, whoa, whoa. I never said I'd take medication. I'm not signing up to be some sort of emotionless zombie."

Dr. Brown's expression flickered with frustration and then returned to the unaffected demeanor he'd maintained before.

"Medication can help, Chastity. Let's not forget *you're* in control here. If you don't like the way something makes you feel, then we stop it and lower the dosage or switch to something else. You tell me how you're feeling and how you'd *like* to feel, and then we can move toward that goal together. Nobody is forcing you to take medication… just like no one is gonna stop you from leaving. You are here voluntarily. My patients come here to make their lives better, not worse. That's all I am interested in. Now that your diagnosis has been re-confirmed, *you* get to decide how your future looks."

Chastity nodded and snatched her purse from the floor beside her. "I need some time to think about all of this."

"Absolutely. I completely understand." He pressed a button on his keyboard and spun to face her. "I've sent all three prescriptions to the pharmacy you put on file. They're all low doses.

If you decide to give them a try, we can go up or down as you see fit once you decide to give them a whirl."

She nodded and slung her suede purse over her shoulder. "Okay."

"Oh, and one more thing. If a depressive bout hits and you need help, please call me here at the office. Reach out. My door never closes for patients. Even the stubborn ones." He smiled. "If I'm not immediately available, leave a message with my staff, and I'll return your call."

Despite his clinical disposition, Chastity saw the glint of humanity in his eyes, a disarming warmth that made her realize he wasn't out to beat her down about her impulsive past. It had been him, and *only* him, who offered her the option for a wildly different future.

31

Barrett sat in the department store parking lot as his Jeep idled and his fuel light blazed. The gas station would be the next stop. He flipped through his contacts, spotted Will's name, and fired off a text message.

> **BARRETT: Get a sitter. You and Ava are coming out with us tonight. And no wedding talk.**

He called Chastity, eager to hear her voice. His body was excited at the idea of soon feeling her skin, tasting her tongue. His stomach leaped as he waited for her to answer.

One ring.

Two.

Then, suddenly, the phone clicked to life with a stuffy-nosed Chastity answering on the other end.

"Barrett?" her voice dripped with pain, tone wavering on the fine edge of a sob.

"Chastity, what's wrong? Are you okay?" he asked, heart crashing into the hard floor of his gut.

"They know."

"Who knows? Knows what?"

"They found out."

"Aphrodite, you're going to have to give me more than that." Barrett's eyebrows furrowed as he stared out the windshield.

"Someone told my parents we were dating and what you do. Like, what you *really* do." She sobbed briefly before pulling herself back together. "They said I embarrassed the family." A sob escaped her taut throat, and she inhaled a ragged breath. "They disowned me, Barrett!"

"Oh, Chastity." His heart ached for her, knowing all too well what it felt like to suddenly lose your parents. Chastity's parents were intentionally turning their back on her. It was a *choice*. He considered that might even somehow feel worse.

"If you don't want to see me anymore, and make amends with your folks..." He couldn't even finish the thought. His brain screamed at him to shut his mouth. The mere thought of not seeing her again felt like pulling out his own beating heart and squeezing it with an iron fist.

The thought of having to part ways with his Aphrodite over something so *stupid* pissed him off. She should never have been put in a position to choose. He refused to add to her torment.

"*You're* not the problem. My *job* is not the problem. It's *their* judgmental attitude and this holier-than-thou bullshit that is the *problem*."

"They have *never* tried to understand me, Barrett. They never *wanted* to. And for that, I don't think there's any fixing this."

"Chastity, you are something wonderful, and you don't deserve any of this. Also… fuck your parents."

"I really wish I could just hold you and tell you this stupid shit will pass."

"Thank you." She sniffled. "Are you still doing the get-together tonight?"

"Yeah. But you don't have to… If you need time and space…"

"I just really don't want to be alone right now," she cried.

"Then, yes. I'll pick you up in a little bit. Okay?"

"Can I…?"

"What?"

"If Will and them are coming, can I invite Sherri?"

"Sherri?"

"Mrs. Nussbaum." She sniffled again. She sounded like a sad child.

He chuckled warmly. "Of course, baby. Of course. You can invite whoever you want. I'm sure she'd like that. You two can catch up on *Summer Fling*."

"*Summer Love*," she corrected, followed by a small laugh.

"Alright, pick you up in a bit. I lo—" he stopped abruptly, mid-word, "I love to hear you laugh."

"Thanks for cheering me up, Barrett."

"I'll see you tonight."

As he hung up, Barrett panicked. Those three terrifying words he'd almost uttered lolled around his mouth like sugary candies. He swallowed them down, skin on fire, neck growing hot as the terrifying reality of how he truly felt for her set in.

I'm in deep shit, he thought.

32

The evening air was chilly as Barrett put the finishing touches on the fire pit, an imperfect circle dug into the sandy shoreline a few feet in diameter, far away from the shrubbery surrounding Jackson Lake. Tenting the last of the firewood in the center, he looked up at the blanket of stars above them.

The night was uncharacteristically calm for this time of year. Summer warmth seemed to be edging itself closer as the frigid winter nights gradually shifted to a temperature most Wyomingites considered comfortable.

Feeling around in the pockets of his blue zippered hoodie, Barrett produced a match, lit it, and flicked it in the pit at the gasoline-soaked wood. A *whoosh* of fire rose in front of his face, forcing him to take a step back.

He recalled dozens of parties in his youth on this lake. Every nook and cranny had a memory. He'd had sex with his high school girlfriend behind a nearby tree where they'd carved their initials, only to scratch them out a week later. There were familiar bushes he'd thrown up behind and patches of dirt where he'd stared for hours, drunkenly trying to find all the constellations. The memories felt like wearing a favorite old sweater, warm from the dryer.

In the distance, a set of headlights came his direction, winding down the dirt path and heading toward him, kicking up a dusty plume in its wake. Another vehicle's headlights sliced through the cloud, followed by another still. Within a few minutes, they'd all circled the pit and killed their engines, tailgates facing the roaring fire.

Chastity was the first to amble out, quickly jogging toward Barrett. Twisted curls bounced against her shoulders, vibrant hair colors muted in the moon and firelight. He admired the shapely legs jutting out of her white shorts and the jiggle of her bra-less breasts as she bounded closer.

Holding open his arms, Barrett welcomed her in. Without hesitation, she crashed into him, her weight a pleasant pressure against his chest. Catching her without so much as a grunt, Barrett spun her around. Her soft giggle vibrated against his neck. Setting her down, he tilted her chin, lifting her eyes in the direction of his own. Her puffy bags and red nose stirred a fiercely protective feeling in him. Her heart had broken, and he wanted to soothe it, to be a balm on all that ached within her.

He couldn't fix the past, the words exchanged between Chastity and her parents, and he felt wholly responsible for their divide. He knew, more than anyone, to feel the absence of both parents in an instant.

His eyes bore into hers, thumbs stroking her cheeks. "I'm so sorry that I caused this."

"What? No," she said. "We haven't seen eye to eye in a long time. They never tried to, and now I don't have to force it anymore. It hurts, but it's not your fault. It's *them*. Not *us*."

Us.

He swallowed hard. He had never really been part of an *us* before. *Not like this.*

She planted a soft kiss on his lips, then one on the tip of his nose. "I don't want to think about them anymore tonight. I just want to be here with you."

He nodded, kissing her forehead. Will and Ava laid a blanket down and sat in the bed of Will's maroon pickup. They were dressed in almost identical hoodies and sweatpants.

Barrett laughed. "Nice outfits. Is *Neiderman's* having a big two-for-one sale?"

"She doesn't need to wear anything special to be the sexiest woman alive," Will said, putting his arm around his fiancee.

"In my defense," Ava said, "Will didn't didn't say anything about anyone else being here. I was supposed to be prepping *save the dates* tonight."

"So glad you could *find the time*, then," Barrett joked.

"Thankfully, she's a take-charge kinda woman. Otherwise, I'd have just eloped with her and had a small wedding on a beach somewhere."

"Is that still an option?" she joked, trying to tame her frizzed auburn hair.

"So glad I found the place on the first try. I was worried I was going to get lost out here and eaten by wolves or something." Sherri Nussbaum, the oldest in the group by a decade, adjusted her black V-neck sweater and high-rise denim pants. Chastity bolted away to greet her with a hug.

"Sherri, so glad you could make it. Let me introduce you to everyone." She pointed around at the group accordingly. "Will and Ava, Barrett, of course. This is my friend Rachel…"

Rachel waved politely and approached the fire. Barrett smiled, remembering her as Chastity's ride from the police station. Her cherry-wood-colored hair looked black in the moonlight, tied up in a ponytail, tube top barely covering her large breasts, exposing her flat belly. A few weeks ago, Barrett would have looked at her shorts and impractical wedge sandals and tried to get her out of both as fast as possible. But meeting Chastity felt like it changed everything.

Another vehicle pulled down the road and approached the campfire, doing a clumsy nine-point turn to get her car's trunk to face the fire, too.

She stepped out and waved timidly. "I made it!"

Will chuckled and tilted his head. "Well! Who do we have here?"

"I'm Maya. *Aguilar*."

"Oh!" There was recognition in Will's eyes.

Ava perked up. "Oh my God, a client! Have you come to complain about Barrett's service? He's still a little rough around the edges, but we have faith that he will improve."

Maya laughed. "Zero complaints. Mr. Andrews here just basically forced me to come out for a night to clear my head."

Barrett waved her closer for a hug. She wobbled to him in her tennis shoes, firelight flickering against her patterned sundress. He squeezed her tight and invited her to join them on the back edge of his Jeep.

Chastity elbowed Barrett, and he shot back up to his feet. "My apologies. For those of you who maybe don't really know her yet, this is my girlfriend, Chastity."

Ava gasped, and Chastity's own eyes widened in surprise at the label.

"Girlfriend? Wow," Will said. "Never thought I'd see the day."

"Don't make it *weird*," Barrett joked.

"Oh, it's weird, alright," Ava offered with a snort. She turned to Chastity. "Darling, you're beautiful. What the hell do you see in this oaf? Wait… blink twice if he's holding you hostage."

"You guys are dicks," Barrett teased. Then he pointed to Maya, addressing Ava. "She's a workaholic too. She's like a nicer, quieter version of you."

"I'm plenty nice, just not to boyish man-children like you," Ava said with a sarcastic grin.

Barrett tugged a large igloo cooler toward him and pulled out two chilled bottles of booze and a few bottles of water. "There's whiskey if anyone wants some. Honey and regular."

"You got cups?" Ava asked.

"Nope. Gonna have to deal with my cooties."

"Oh God. *Cooties*." Ava giggled. "You really *are* a man-child."

He took a swig. The liquid burned like fire as it went down, spreading across his abdomen like a bomb in his empty stomach.

"That's my one and only drink tonight, you guys. *Designated Driver Barrett* is now officially at your service."

Chastity snatched the bottle from Barrett and took a swig, which was made more delicious after knowing Barrett's lips had been wrapped around it only moments before.

"Let's start things off with a game, shall we? A little icebreaker, perhaps. How about a little truth-or-dare?"

In unison, everyone else groaned.

"You kidding me? That's a good game," Barrett hollered.

"Cooties and now truth-or-dare?" Chastity joked, leaning away from him like he was contagious. "I'm gonna need to see some ID. Are you old enough to drink, boy?"

"Alright, smarty-pants. What would *you* suggest?"

"Truth-or-*drink*. You gotta hand the bottle to the person of your choice. They can choose to answer something truthfully about themselves, or they have to take a drink."

"What's the difference?" Barrett asked with a sassy bobble of his head.

Will interjected before Chastity could answer. "The difference is you can't give Sherri hypothermia by telling her to skinny-dip in the lake or get Will arrested for running naked down the highway screaming 'I'm bigfoot' on some dumb dare.'"

"How about another rule," Sherri said, her tone more commanding than the others. "No photos? I don't need anything embarrassing coming back on me or my family. They think I'm at a fundraiser right now."

Barrett shrugged. "Sounds good. Chastity's game, so she should start." He tickled her on the side. She shrieked and jumped away from the Jeep to get away.

"Fine. Maya?"

Maya lifted her head from picking at her cuticles. She shifted uncomfortably on her trunk.

"Oh, no. I don't want to start."

"Please? Chastity plead, handing Maya the bottle of whisky.

"Truth, I guess." Maya eyed the bottle in her hands like it was ready to bite her.

"What's one thing you're *really* good at?" Chastity asked, voice soft with the clearly anxious woman.

"Uh... I don't know. Work, I guess?"

Barrett groaned. "Come on, Maya. I know there's more to you than C++."

She smiled weakly. "I... I've always been decent at art. I used to doodle a lot in school because I was bored. I still do at work sometimes to keep myself from falling asleep during meetings. I just pretend like I am taking really detailed notes and nod along."

Everyone chuckled.

Maya pointed the bottle at Sherri. "You."

Sherri swallowed a lump of nerves and fiddled with the cuffs of her sweater. "Oh boy. Truth."

Maya laughed. "Why are you hanging out with these weirdos?"

Sherri chuckled a little. "I don't get out much. I'm always hosting charity events and the like, so there isn't much time for stuff like this."

Barrett tossed another hunk of wood on the fire from the back of his Jeep, sending up a cloud of glittering sparks before dying down again.

"Your turn to ask, Sherri," Chastity said.

"Um, hmmm, Will, I guess."

"Truth. I have too much to do tomorrow to be dealing with a hangover," he snickered.

"*Pussy*," Barrett mumbled with a smile.

"Are you a maid, too, Will?" Maya asked.

"Yeah," He laughed. "I'm the O.G. maid of this crew, actually. Barrett joined my fleet a couple weeks back."

"Fleet? Really? It's just the two of us," Barrett said.

"We're in the process of hiring two more right now, Mr. Know-it-all." Will turned back to the ladies. "And, yes, *Man Maid* is mine… and

Ava's. Been up and running for about, what, three years now?"

Ava nodded confirmation. "Two and three quarters."

Will spoke. "Chastity. You're up."

"Truth," the rainbow-haired woman said brazenly, without hesitation, "*and* drink."

"That's my girl," Barrett said, pulling her closer as she took a drink from the second bottle.

"How'd you meet Barrett?"

"At a bar. A guy who'd bought me a drink was being pushy. Barrett pretended to be my boyfriend. Now," she held his hand, "after his little introduction, I guess we don't have to *pretend* anymore."

"Rachel, you're up. Truth or drink? Will asked.

"Draaaaaaank!" Rachael said eagerly, bouncing on the trunk so hard that the car shook. She took a long sip with a stone-still expression. "I choose Will."

"It was just my turn!"

"Well, now it's your turn again!" Rachel playfully yelled. "What do you love the most about your fiancee?"

Everyone laughed.

"There are right and wrong answers, Will," Ava said, pretending to be stern.

Will exhaled. "Shit, I'll give you a list of five things right now." Will grabbed Ava's hand and smiled. "I love her drive. She's the hardest-working woman I've ever met. I love her *fire* and everything, good and bad, that comes with it. I love the way she is with my daughter. I love how beautiful she is. She stole my heart from day one. And, well, number five, it wouldn't be decent to talk about in public."

The women in the group *ooohed* as Barrett faked a gag.

"Sorry, you guys. This game's a little junior high for my taste." Rachel dug in her purse and pulled out a white, hand-rolled joint the size of a cigarette. "Anyone mind if I smoke some of the ol' sticky-icky?"

Everyone slowly shook their heads, and she lit the end with a bedazzled lighter. She sputtered out a cough and smiled, offering it to the others. "It's not much, but everyone's welcome."

Will shook his head. "No. None for me. Weed and I don't mix."

"Willing parties only," Rachel said.

Maya took it, sucking down a few deep drags like she had missed it. "Oh, you angel! It's illegal here still, right?" Maya asked quietly.

Rachel nodded. "So don't narc on me."

"Where the hell did you get it? I haven't been able to find any to save my life. All they have around here is that Delta-eight shit."

"A friend of mine, a guy from the club, always goes down to Colorado for work. He brings it back for me."

Maya took another puff and offered it to Sherri.

"I haven't smoked since college," she said hesitantly as the joint smoldered in her hand. She took a drag and started coughing as soon as the smoke hit her lungs. She handed it back to Maya, doubling over as she continued her coughing fit. "Bit... rusty... I guess."

Ava hopped off the truck bed and strolled over, Will watching from his seat, eyebrows raised, a look of surprise etched into his features. She reached her fingers out to Maya. "May I?"

Maya handed it off, and Ava took it, taking a long drag. "Man, that takes me back. Why the hell did we stop doing stuff like this? When the hell did we all grow up?"

She held the joint out to Barrett, and he shook his head. "Normally yes, but... I just offered to be DD."

"Chastity?" Ava held her hand out.

Chastity swallowed and gave a nervous chuckle, her face suddenly looking a little pained. "I love it. But it messes with me."

"That's kind of the point, isn't it?" Ava smiled.

Chastity looked at the fire, liquid courage in her veins tipping over the pitcher of emotion overflowing in her chest. The words came rushing out, sounding like they were screamed through a megaphone in her own head.

"I'm bipolar."

There was a moment of silence. Barrett rubbed her back reassuringly. Unable to make eye contact with anyone, Chastity lifted her gaze up to a moonless sky, its normally steadfast presence somehow abandoning her in her time of need.

"Drugs and booze really hit me differently, I'm realizing. Sometimes the weed makes me mellow, and sometimes it takes away the last fuck I have to give. I flunked out of veterinary school a few months ago because I was high and manic, always feeling ten-foot-tall-and-bulletproof, trying to self-medicate on anything and everything I could get my hands on. I was diagnosed a couple months ago, and I couldn't handle it."

The area was quiet save for the crackling wood in the fire and the gentle sounds of the lake a few feet away.

"I promise I'm not a danger. I'm just… scared. You and my parents are the only people I've told, and they didn't take it well."

At the mention of her parents, tears formed in her eyes. Her body slumped, and she wiped her cheeks with her palms.

"That's fucked up. What did your parents actually say?" Rachel asked gently before taking another puff.

"My father said nothing. My mother gave me a lecture insinuating that this was brought on by my lifestyle and wild ways. She insisted it was something I'd grow out of if I'd just try harder to get my life together. She told me to pray for strength. For '*this too shall pass*.'"

The tears came faster, dribbling down her chin to her neck. "I overheard her and her friends talking shit about me the day I moved out. And then tonight she called, said they found out about what Barrett does for a living, and that we're together now. She said they're ashamed of me, that until I can come to my senses and stop seeing Barrett and stop with this 'bipolar nonsense,' they refuse to be seen with me. Like their fucking *reputation* means more than their own daughter."

The others sat in silence.

Chastity sobbed again. "I'm sorry. I know that was more than a little bit of an overshare."

"Girl, most of us have issues these days. Our parents had them, too. They just didn't have names for them. They didn't have a DSM-V or WebMD or a lot of counselors or therapists like we do now. Hell, I'm on a bunch of shit for my generalized anxiety disorder. And I swear to God, if one more person tells me to relax or do yoga, I'm gonna snap."

Chastity sniffled, letting out an involuntary laugh. She shivered, and without hesitating, Barrett took off his hoodie and wrapped it around her shoulders. She flashed him a grateful expression.

Rachel exhaled. "I've had ADHD since I was a kid. I take meds for it, but I don't tell people because everyone wants to buy my Adderall from me. Either that, or they think I'm *faking it* because I still function without medication. We are all a little fucked up. And with you, that sucks about your folks because you didn't just *pick this up* from someone. It isn't *chlamydia*. You've probably had it a long time and didn't know. You're still a badass."

"Most badass woman *I've* ever met," Barrett said, resting his cheek on her head.

Will and Ava smiled at him like proud parents watching their child take their first steps.

Will leaned toward the fire. "He's a good guy, Chastity. A bit of a jackass sometimes, but if anyone can handle him, a tough sumbitch like *you* can."

***

As the fire died and their friends packed up for the evening, Barrett pulled Chastity to the front of his Jeep, stealing a moment while the others were distracted.

"What?" Chastity asked, confused.

He pinned her to the grill, grasped her neck, and kissed her with a fervor that surprised her. His hand slipped up her shorts, between her legs, grazing the fabric of her panties. She quietly groaned against his mouth, squirming against his hand.

"You look sexy in my hoodie." His hand retreated from her thighs and gently pinched her nipple piercing through the thin fabric of her shirt until her eyes fluttered.

"*What do you say we get the fuck out of here and have ourselves a proper sleepover?*" Barrett whispered into her ear. "*Maybe finish what we started on the mountain yesterday?*"

Chastity cupped the bulge in his pants, rising on her toes to kiss him with enough passion to give him a clear answer. She tugged his lip between her teeth and released it as she stepped away.

"Drive fast."

"You got it." He slapped her on the ass, and she yipped, climbing into his passenger seat. "Just not *too* fast," he joked. "I'm in a *teensy* bit of hot water with the police around here lately."

33

As soon as the door pushed open, Barrett hung his keys on the jackalope and hoisted Chastity in the air, wrapping her bare legs around his waist as he carried her to the bathroom. Her rainbow locks caressed his cheeks as their hungry mouths collided, tongues skillfully flicking at one another.

In seconds, he had spun the faucet dial and set her down on the counter as hot steam filled the tiny room.

She stripped off his shirt, scrambling for his belt, tugging the buckle, and ripping the leather strap from the loops. She wrapped it over him, using it like reins to pull him in between her parted legs.

The look of lust in her eyes had a hint of something darker, and that desire made him hard. He unzipped, pushing his pants and underwear to the floor. Her eyes settled on his dick, and she smiled. He yanked off her shirt, freeing her breasts, sensitive nipples pierced through with horizontal bars. In seconds, he'd yanked her free of her skimpy shorts, and she sat naked and beautiful in front of him.

He pulled her roughly into the shower, pressing her against the tile wall gently by her throat as the delightfully hot water soothed her chilled skin.

Barrett closed the glass door and growled into her ear. "You're a *dirty* girl, Aphrodite."

He pressed his hard cock against her thigh, feeling the hot water rush over them both. "Let's get you clean."

He released her and she grinned as he squirted a liberal amount of shampoo in his hand. He spun her around, working it through her rainbow tresses, watching the bubbly suds dribble down the curves of her breasts.

He used the rest on himself, lathering quickly. She felt turned on, watching him rub circles on his scalp, watching rivulets of water trickle down the deep-cut grooves of his body, admiring the sloped paths they took through the muscular "V" of his pelvis.

They rinsed, and she leaned into him, breasts pressed against his chest as she massaged conditioner into their hair. Squirting some in her own hand, she gripped his cock. His head rolled back, savoring the sensation as she slipped her fist back and forth around his shaft.

As soon as they rinsed, he spun her again and slowly shoved her against the other wall, holding her there below the showerhead.

He hoisted her up again with ease, wrapping her legs around his hips, positioning the head of his dick at her entrance, eager to dip inside. He cupped her jaw and pressed her harder into the tile. He growled into her ear, "Do you want me?"

"More than anything," she panted through the force of his hand, one holding her tight enough to restrict her movement but not too tight to breathe.

"*Tell me you want me to fuck you.*"

"*I want you to fuck me,*" she said, pressing her back hard against the wall, trying to use it as leverage to tilt her pelvis toward him, wanting to feel him sink inside.

He shot his own hips back, not allowing her to call the shots. "*Bad girl.* You know what I want to hear."

She grinned and defiantly bucked her hips again, finally relenting. "This pussy is all yours."

With that, he groaned and, like he had all of the time in the world, he slipped inside of her slowly, deliberately, giving her every thick inch of himself.

She moaned long and loud. With his free hand, he slid the frosted door open and turned her head with the other, forcing her to look at herself in the bathroom mirror.

"I want you to watch yourself. I want you to see in your pretty little face what my fucking cock does to your body when I'm inside you."

Her eyes fluttered. His dirty talk was driving her wild, his cock filling her up. She squirmed, trying her best to milk an orgasm from his body.

"No. You don't fuck me. I fuck *you*. Understand me, Aphrodite?"

She nodded, face pink beneath his firm grasp.

"I want you to watch me fuck that pretty little cunt of yours."

She watched intently as he fucked her hard against a wall of white tile. With every plunge of his hips in the mirror, she transcended to a new level of pleasure. She watched as the sight of her own orgasm made her shudder even harder. When she did, he released her and quickened his pace. She caressed Barrett's tensed neck muscles in their reflection, eyes never straying from the glass as he came inside of her.

34

Chastity lay on the pillow next to Barrett's, watching the steady rise and fall of his chest, his body utterly relaxed and depleted. Her core ached from a long night featuring multiple rounds of sex.

No, not sex.

By the end, there had been something more. Something that felt intimate and gentle yet powerful in a strangely unknown way.

There had been something that felt like *love.*

The prospect of love... *real* love... *true* love... made her overjoyed and sick to her stomach simultaneously. She was in a free fall, unsure where she would land and what her ultimate destiny might be. Tears welled as she thought about a future with him, trying to balance pleasing another person and discovering herself at the same time, a delicate balance, to say the least.

She wondered about the medication her therapist had suggested and felt a swell of guilt.

Barrett had chosen to be with her as she was, but what if she decided to take the medication to balance the intoxicating mania and devastating lows?

What if it changed her?

What if she became something he didn't recognize or *like*?

Would she be the same person?

Would it be fair to drag such a new relationship and a caring man through it all?

Would it be fair to show someone one side of you, to let them fall deeply for that person, only to radically change later?

He hadn't yet seen the endless hours of sleeping, the depression that impeded her basic ability to function some days. He hadn't watched her scrounge her way out of a crushing level of debt, debt she put herself in with impulsive spending to temporarily alleviate bouts of sadness.

The psychiatrist said it would take time to dial in the medication and that it would be a challenging few months getting started.

Would this gorgeous man, who could have his pick of any woman in a thousand-mile radius, stick around to see her through it all?

She thought back to the look in his eyes when he was inside of her in the shower. It wasn't the look you give a one-night-stand, she should know. It was *more*.

Laying back, she peered through his skylight at an endless sea of stars, feeling jealous of them all. Stars didn't have an impossible decision to make. They could merely *exist*.

Tears drenched the pillow as she turned back to his sleeping face, memorizing every inch of his face. She had made her decision. And it was the hardest thing she would ever have to do.

35

When Barrett awoke, he stared out his skylight at a dawn sky feathered in magenta and indigo, struck by the pleasant notion that, for the first time in many years, he was not waking up alone.

Reaching the other side of the bed, his hand fell through the space where Chastity should have been, patting fabric no longer warm from the touch of her body, now cold, vacant. The idea that she might have once again fled in the night without so much as a goodbye physically pained him.

Before his mind could wander further, he heard the sound of feet pattering against the wood floor on the other side of the studio apartment. He wiped his hands down his face, feeling the drain from the long night of meaningful sex that had wrung every ounce of energy from his body.

He grabbed a pair of boxers from his dresser and slid them on. As he did, he saw Chastity pacing in front of the wall of windows. He approached, seeing her lost in thought, watching the sparkle of sunlight dance off her tear-streaked cheeks.

"Chastity?"

She jerked her head in his direction, face heartbroken and distraught. Whatever it was that was bothering her, his brain wanted to wrestle it into submission, inflicting ten times her pain on whoever made her feel like this.

"What's wrong, baby? Is it... your parents?"

Chastity shook her head, crossing her arms over her breasts, now covered in one of his wrinkled T-shirts. Under different circumstances, he would be turned on seeing her wearing his clothes with nothing beneath them. But her swollen eyes made him upset.

She turned, and he wrapped his arms around her. A sob broke free from her chest as she clung to his shoulders, pulling him closer.

"Did I do something wrong?"

Again, she shook her head, body weak in his fatigued arms. Gently, he tilted her chin up. Her skin was soaked with tears.

"Talk to me."

After a moment of silent contemplation, she uttered the words she knew she would replay in her head for months, if not years, with a sad regret.

"I can't do this."

His heart sank.

Her eyes and her tone made it clear she had made up her mind. He could feel her warmth slipping away.

"I don't understand. What did I do?" he asked frantically, holding her hand to his chest. "Let me fix it. Whatever it is, I can fix it."

"You can't fix it. It's not yours to fix, Barrett. You didn't do anything wrong." She sobbed.

"Please... talk to me, Chastity."

She straightened her back and looked at him, eyes suddenly hard. "Barrett, I care about you. I really do. But... it's not the right time for this. For... us."

He nodded, trying to retain some dignity. "Alright. What is this about, Chastity?"

She forced her tone to stay even. "I have to make some really difficult decisions. About my life. About my bipolar and my medications. About my career and my future. Barrett," a tear fell from her eye, "I can't be your girlfriend... because I don't even know who I *am*."

"That's—"

"Barrett, you haven't seen the real *lows*. You have *barely* seen me in my highs. I'm in debt, did you know that? When I am manic, I spend. I know now that I was manic at college. Now, I can feel myself on the down-slide. This is going to be rough. I *have* to do something. I *want* to do something so I can one day have a life like *this*, somewhere in that sweet spot between Heaven and Hell. But, until then, I'm in this bipolar purgatory, endlessly bouncing between the two. I can't hide from it anymore. I don't *want* to. I want to explore what is out there so that I can feel better and make a real life out of all this mess. But it'll take some time. It's not an overnight fix. I don't expect you to wait around for that. I don't even know if I'll be the same me when it's all done."

She squeezed his hand, and the angered look on his face softened.

"I'm absolutely terrified, Barrett. I can't be who you need me to be or who you think I already am. I can't be who I want to be... for *you*. I just lost my parents. The thought of diving headfirst into a real relationship and then losing you is unbearable."

"You wouldn't *lose* me. I'm here. I want you. I want all the fucked-up-ness that might come with you."

That made her laugh. She sniffled, and then she frowned and sobbed into the back of her hand.

"Chastity, if you don't want this right now... it fucking crushes me, but I can respect that. I care about you. But... please, baby, don't shut me out completely. I'd rather be around you, helping you through this, than just have this empty Aphrodite-sized void. I'll give you all the space you want, but please don't count me out completely. You could use someone cheering you on from the stands, even if you want to just be... friends... or whatever. Just let me be there for you."

With tears streaming down her cheeks, she nodded.

"I am so sorry, Barrett."

"Don't be." He fought the tears in his own eyes. "I'm not sorry about our time together. I don't regret a *second* of this. Take the time you need, but know I'm here. You don't have to do everything alone."

"Thank you."

He shook his head and mustered a sad laugh.

"What?" She wiped her face.

"You really are so stubborn, you know that?" His heart broke a little as the words left his mouth.

They dressed in silence, and Barrett drove her back to the *Rabbit Run* apartments without uttering a single word.

What could he possibly say?

Her decision felt firm. Decisive. Painful and wise in equal measure. She needed to get her shit together, a feeling Barrett was all-too-familiar with.

As he walked her to the complex doors, he wrapped his arms around her, eager to feel her body against his for just a moment longer. The more he wanted to hold her, to embrace her tightly, to beg for her to change her mind... the more he knew he shouldn't. Love was wild and feral, like Smoky. He knew that the harder he held it, the faster it would all just slip through his fingers.

As he sat in his Jeep, engine purring, he wished he had told her what he felt, the ones he had never uttered to a woman before.

I love you.

Maybe he had missed his chance.

Whether he said them or not, the sentiment was true.

He was in love with her. And for a moment, she had been his to cherish, his to cling to, and that had to be worth something, some small consolation.

Maybe this wouldn't be permanent. Maybe, like Smoky, if he kept the window open, she would one day return and stay a while.

36

The heat of the brutal mid-summer sun was partially blocked by the building with a stone facade in front of Barrett's idling Jeep. He watched the double doors, waiting for the familiar face to emerge.

Will's voice came through the car speakers. "So what do you think? Are you up for it?"

Barrett sighed, gut twisting at the prospect. "Denver? Jesus, Will, that's a huge ask."

"I know, Barrett. I just figured, with your Gam-Gam gone now, it might be time for a change of scenery and a sizeable pay-bump in your salary."

"But Denver? Will, why there? It's a bunch of woke potheads who stress pronouns and eat runny eggs on their burgers."

"I know, Barrett."

"You're not listening to me, Will!" Barrett was shouting now. "I *said* they put *eggs* on their *burgers*. How do you not find that offensive?"

"Just wait til you try their alleged Tex-Mex fusion shit. I'm not saying… you can't… you don't go to Denver for the fucking *cuisine*,

Barrett." Will was so flustered and stressed that he was stammering.

"Why can't you and Ava go to set up the new branch?"

"Because we have a daughter, Barrett. Remember your Goddaughter, Starla? Hmmm? She's established in a school and ballet and extra-curricular activities. I'm not going to uproot her for something like this if I don't have to. She's got friends here. Her whole life is here. I can't ask an eight-year-old to give all of that up so Daddy can branch out and set up a new fleet for a few months. Not to mention, we are about to get *married* soon."

He'd heard rumblings about Denver for a few weeks. Chatter in the main office. Spreadsheets printed by Ava lying around.

Deep down, Barrett had already known the answer before Will had even asked him to relocate, but he'd needed more time. Time to make up a plausible excuse. Time to scramble for a reason not to go.

After losing his grandmother at the beginning of the summer, he was excited at the prospect of a fresh place to start over. New sights and experiences. A new start where he had no reputation, no local douchebags with old high school grudges wanting to fight him, no bitterly-scorned lovers, and a chance to hire his own muscular crew at a job he enjoyed.

He had every reason to leave.

All but *one*.

As if she had a sixth sense, summoned by Barrett's thoughts, Chastity walked out the automatic doors of the Harmony Institute, bouncing in a red tulip skirt and white tank, looking like fucking *sex incarnate*.

His hands itched, wanting to tug the waistband of that skirt until it was around her ankles, where it *belonged*. He imagined her bare ass, full and firm, in the black lace thong he remembered so vividly.

"Barrett, did I lose you?" Will's voice interrupted his dirty thoughts.

Focusing on anything but the mental image of Chastity naked would take a real concerted effort on a day like today, on a day when she was so close but totally out of bounds.

For a while, being friends was enough. At least she was still in his life, and he in hers. But as the months passed, his heart ached at the thought that when she started dating again, that it might not be with him.

He knew that if that happened, he couldn't stand by and watch, pretending to be happy that she was with someone else as he stayed downgraded to some friend zone.

Maybe it was better to go to someplace with eggs on burgers than to sit around and be made to look like a fool. His heart had already broken for her once.

Twice might break him completely.

She grinned at him through the windshield, and he waved, trying his best to hide the sadness in his smile.

"Nah, man. I'm still here. I'll do it. Tell Ava I'm in."

"Thank you, man. Starla thanks you. My future marriage thanks you... I owe you *big* for this."

With a snort, Barrett looked at his phone in the mount on his dashboard. "Yeah, you do. But make the checks fat enough, and I'll dry my tears with dollar bills."

"I gotta run. Ava will get you set up with everything. We'll cover relocation expenses. You'll be golden, Pony-boy," Will said.

Chastity pulled open the car door and hopped in.

Barrett cleared his throat, "Alright, catch you later, Will."

"Oh! Hi, Will!" Chastity chirped.

"Oh... hey, Chastity! How are things goin' on your end?"

"Great. Feeling good! *Helluva* lot better now that the docs and I've gotten the meds balanced."

"You guys out running errands together?" Will asked. "If you *are*, make sure to pick him up a hamper so he has a place to finally put all his dirty clothes. The irony of someone cleaning houses for a living and—"

"Hey, I thought you had to go, wise-ass," Barrett said, rolling his eyes.

"No. Not running a bunch of errands. My car's in the shop right now. Barrett offered to drive me to my therapy appointment today. Isn't he sweet?"

Will laughed, "Yeah, *a real cupcake*, that one. Okay… I'll let you two get on with your day. Congrats. I'm real glad you're doin' well. Take care, Sweetie."

"Thanks, Will," she said.

"Later, Chode," Barrett said, throwing a peace sign at his phone.

A laugh erupted on the other side. "Bye, Dickweed. Keep an eye out for Ava's emails. I'm sure you're about to get a barrage of them."

"Will do." Barrett ended the call. He did his best to muster a smile. "Let's grab some grub before all this hard labor."

She rolled her eyes. "You're assembling a dining set from Ikea. It's not like I'm asking you to haul bags of cement."

"Have you ever put together anything from Ikea? The hard labor isn't physical. It's a mental challenge. Building furniture from there is like trying to solve a Rubix cube."

She grabbed his hand and gave him a warm smile, laying the side of her head against the backrest. "Thank you for waiting. I got really good news, but I'll tell you over dinner."

He loved her like this.

Relaxed. At ease.

Happy.

Not manic, but… happy.

Over the last few months, he watched from the sidelines, heart thrumming every time they were near each other, chest aching when they were apart. His apartment felt empty, her smell lingering on his bedding for weeks after she'd made him a broken man. The warmth and sass she oozed had hopelessly tethered him to her, stringing him along as he twisted in the wind, never sure if *their time* would ever come again.

Now, it was too late.

He wouldn't be around long enough to afford another chance.

The thump in his chest beat its swan song for a love that could have been but never would be again.

"Yeah." Barrett gave her hand a squeeze and then let it go to put the car in drive. "I have a lot to tell you, too."

37

With fried chicken in tow, Chastity and Barrett settled around the small kitchen bar in her apartment, an apartment where they had spent dozens of nights watching movies, building furniture, and hanging new art where there once had been marker-scribbled graffiti.

Molly, Chastity's three-legged Mastiff, romped through the tiny space, plowing into Barrett and offering bountiful kisses and happy whines.

"She likes you more than she likes me, I swear." Chastity laughed, reaching into the fridge. She snatched a soda and one of the craft beers that she kept on hand for Barrett.

He set the bags on the laminate countertop and glanced around her kitchen. Molly sniffed their bounty, which was nearly at eye level.

"Shit is so shiny in here it hurts my eyes to look at. Even the grout looks better. Someone has been cleanin' her cute little ass off."

Chastity shoved the beer into his chest, knocking some air from his lungs. "It's amazing what you will resort to when you're bored and trying to pay off your credit cards."

Cracking open her can, she took a sip as the foam nearly spilled over. Smacking her lips, she hummed pleasurably, a sound that made Barrett's blood rush south.

"By the way, I paid one off last week. I have one left, and I'll be debt-free, baby!"

Barrett couldn't help but feel a pang of sadness that she wasn't calling him *baby* in a romantic sense.

It didn't matter now, anyway.

The door was shutting on this situation, and now all he had to do was click the handle closed, sealing their fate for good.

"That's amazing!" He fought his emotions, clasping the hand she held up in the air, eyes lingering on each other for a beat too long. He released it and stuffed his fists into the pockets of his jeans, accidentally snagging the fabric of his T-shirt with it.

"Come on. Let's eat in the living room." She snatched her box of chicken tenders and potato wedges. She hopped, hair bobbing as she jogged the short distance to the futon positioned in front of her fifty-inch television screen.

"I saved the season finale of *Summer Love* for us to watch together. Do you realize how much self-control this took? A few months ago, I could have never. Now, please, sit!"

Molly heard the word as her own command and sat in the hallway between the kitchen and the living room.

"Not you, Molly."

As if she understood, Molly stood, wandered over to them, and laid down in front of the futon at their feet.

"I can't believe you saved it for me. Now. This fucking show. I swear to God, if you ever tell anyone I watched this with you... and actually kinda *liked* it... I will deny, deny, deny. I would watch the final episode of *every* season and call and tell you every final match before you're caught up."

She gasped. "That's *diabolical*."

Chastity narrowed her eyes and flipped open her box of chicken. "Men and their sensitive egos."

His eyes raked up her legs as she reached for the TV remote on the end table beside her. He got a flash of the waist strap of her white panties and fought the urge to groan.

"Remind me about the final couples again."

"So Shelly loves Kyle, but Kyle is into Jessica. But Jessica is the *bisexual* girl, so she's into Shelly *and* Bryan. Bryan is the idiot everyone loves and is rooting to win. But he's into *Jessica*, so they might get together. But who knows, she may want Shelly."

Not even vaguely listening, Barrett bit into a potato wedge, watching her in the reflection of the television, how her body moved gracefully, coiled like a cozy snake, oblivious to his gawking.

Knowing the weakest-willed one of the two, Molly propped her head up on the edge of the futon, staring at the fried chicken in Barrett's box.

"Wait," he said, just before Chastity pushed play on the episode. He kicked off his boots and turned on the futon to face her. "You said you had good news."

She tried to hide a smile, forcing her face to stay serious. "I do."

"Shoot," he said through a mouthful of potato.

Molly's eyes traced the path of the fried meat as Barrett lifted a tender to his mouth. Spotting his captive audience, he tossed her a fry, watching her inhale it mid-air.

Chastity took a deep breath. "My psychiatrist said today during our session that it looks like my meds have really balanced out. Overall, I've been doing a lot better. Less impulsive. Got through last month's down-swing,

I'm not crying *nearly* as often as I was. I mean, I still cry… during movies and stuff."

"Or when Kelsey got voted off the island," he added.

"Yeah, but that was different. That elimination wasn't fair. Duke turned around the next day and was flirting with Amy."

"I know. Then, there was the whole *Amy* drama." He gnawed another tender.

"Anyway, I just feel like this weight I never knew existed has been kinda lifted off my shoulders. Like I've been on a treadmill my whole life, and I'm finally getting to step off and take a breather, you know?"

She gave him a genuine smile that warmed his heart. He fought the overwhelming urge to lean forward and kiss her.

"I'm so excited to hear that." His smile wasn't as bright as he was willing it to be. "All I've ever wanted was for you to be happy. I'm so glad you decided to give the medications a shot. You seem less bogged down in the tough times. You're easier to console, and you've been reaching out for help more instead of trying to do it all by yourself."

"That support page changed my life." She smiled again. "The best thing social media ever did was connect us people who are dealing with the same thing together all over the world. Sasha, the girl I met on that page, and I plan to do a movie marathon over Skype soon. She's hilarious. I can't wait for you to meet her. You'll love her. It... it's just such a relief to feel like I'm not alone."

He massaged her shin with his hand, thinking about the word *love* and how he wanted to say it, but not to some stranger named Sasha on a message board.

"You're never alone, Chastity. Not unless you *want* to be."

She nodded. "I know."

He rubbed her leg again and could've sworn he felt goosebumps emerging from beneath his touch.

"So what's next? What's the next step with all of this."

She swallowed, setting her empty box on the table and shooing Molly's nosy snout away from it. Barrett did the same.

"I gotta *live*, I guess. And fuck things up, and fix them, and tweak meds, and then... live some more. Oh, and *therapy*." She chuckled. "I have a *lot* to unpack about my parents still."

"How are things with them going?" he asked, grabbing her foot and massaging it with his hands. She moaned a little, and he felt his dick perk up at the sound of it.

"I dunno. I'm still torn. I'm pissed about the way everything went down."

"Naturally."

"I can't tell if they're apologizing because they saw how fucked-up what they did was or if it just looks bad on them to have a child they don't speak to. They aren't a perfect, happy example of a family if I'm estranged. They haven't agreed to any of the family counseling sessions I offered to set up. So, until then, we might just be at an impasse. Until they can see what I've been struggling with isn't a choice and that you're not a prostitute, I don't know. Judgemental bullshit just doesn't work for me anymore."

"Unless it's people on *Summer Love*."

"Of course." She giggled. The sound made his heart ache.

He would miss that the most.

"What do you think?" she asked, wiggling her other foot to indicate it wanted to be rubbed, too.

He grabbed it and blew out a rush of air as he carefully contemplated his answer. "I just want what is best and healthiest for you. If having that support system in your life makes it better, then I'm all for it. We all make mistakes. And Christians, like everyone else, can be judgemental sometimes, but they can also be the most forgiving, in my experience, too. I just worry that if you're always wondering what your parents are going to think, or they always make you feel judged, then maybe it's best the way that it is. You gotta take care of yourself. And it's not like you *hate* each other. You're just on different paths. You're at least trying to work through it. What they do with that attempt is on them."

Chastity looked up as if the answer was written somewhere in the outdated popcorn ceiling.

"You've seen me through all of this shit. You never judged me. You were never afraid of me, even when I was afraid of myself. Why can't everyone just be like you?"

"Oof," Barrett said. "The thought of that is a nightmare. Can you imagine a bunch of Barrett's running around?"

He faked a shiver, and Chastity laughed.

"Oh, whatever. If people were more like you, the world would have more black eyes but also a lot more compassion and understanding."

"Well, thank you."

"And men would listen more." She smiled at him. "You've always been a great listener."

His heart warmed at the compliment, and he massaged harder, hitting the spot in her arch that turned her body to melting putty.

"That feels incredible. Those heels still aren't broken in yet. They were killing me all afternoon."

His nimble hands moved up, massaging her smooth calves with care and tenderness. He was fully hard now at the touch of her lotioned skin, unsure how he was going to hide the evidence of it with such a rising tent in his pants. He felt like he was in high school all over again.

"What was your news?" she asked, body relaxed, voice like warmed chocolate, smooth and sweet.

"I, um... I'm... moving."

Her eyes shot open, and her body straightened, pulling her leg from his grip. "What... into Gam-Gam's house?"

"No. The Realtor has already found a few potential buyers for that." He hesitated, staring at the carpet. "To... Denver."

Her relaxed smile evaporated.

"Wait, what?"

"I'd heard some rumors the last couple of weeks, but I just got the official word today. *Man Maid* is branching out. Will wants to build a new fleet in a larger metropolitan area. They want me to move down there, hire some guys, and get a client base going."

"Why can't *Will* set it up?"

"He can't leave. He's got the wedding. Plus, Starla is about to start school again. She's got friends and ballet and shit. I don't have all that. Gan-Gam's gone. My lease is up soon. He trusts me. He chose me to go."

She bit her lip, face fraught with frustration. "But… you can't just *leave*."

"Chastity." He leaned forward, clutching one of her hands in his own. "I don't have any of that stuff holding me here."

A tear rolled down Chastity's cheek. "What about *me*?"

His gaze softened. "I can't keep… doing this."

"Doing what?!" Her voice cracked. "You said I'd always have you. I thought you meant it."

"You will! I'll only be a call or a Skype away when you need me."

"This… I don't understand, Barrett."

"Chastity, I can't just pretend that I'm happy being without you."

"But you're not without me. We hang out all the time!"

"Yes, we hang out, but… I don't want to hang out and pretend that I don't *love you*!"

The words silenced them both.

Finally, voice cracking again, he said, "Maybe our time has passed, and I'm just fucking up our friendship by saying that, but I fucking love you. I have for months. This... this is killing me, Chastity. Seeing you and not being able to kiss you or make love to you or fall asleep with you in my arms... it's tearing me apart."

Chastity sat stunned, trying to grasp the gravity of it all.

"I wish that everything you do didn't drive me crazy in the best way, that I didn't want to see you naked every time you're in my sight. I wish that the thought of someone else touching you didn't keep me fucking *awake* at night. I want a life with you that I never wanted with anyone before, and it's *so close*... and I can't have it. It's fucking torture."

He removed her feet from his lap and stood. "I can't do it anymore. I'm sorry. I tried to be a true friend. I really did. But I love you, and this shit twists me up inside. I think the distance could help. You can still call, I can still be there for you from afar, but at least I won't have your feet in my lap pretending touching you is not giving me a raging-fucking-erection. At least I won't have to get a whiff of how goddamn good you always smell or wanna hold you in my arms every time you fall asleep during the *Summer Love* after-show. I won't have to look in your eyes and picture having a *life* with you, a *home*..."

The breath had been sucked out of her lungs. Too many thoughts were racing through her mind at once, struggling to settle on a sentence in rebuttal.

A single word.

Anything.

But nothing came from her lips.

"I should go. I'm sorry."

He dumped his food container in her kitchen trash and stared at it in the bag, wishing he had a bottle of whiskey to crawl into to numb the pain.

"*Don't go.*" It was all she could muster.

He kissed Chastity atop her rainbow-streaked head and left her in silence.

Seconds later, a sob tore from her chest, feeling as though her whole world had just imploded, taking everything good with it.

She rose to her feet and wiped her face. Abandoning her shoes, she sprinted out the door, racing down the hall and stairwell to reach Barrett before it was too late.

"Barrett," Chastity shouted, sprinting out the front door of her apartment complex, bare feet sticking to the hot asphalt.

She waved her hand at his Jeep, one idling in his usual spot in the parking lot.

"Stop, Barrett. Please!"

The warm evening breeze ruffled her hair as she wound her way past several old, dinged-up vehicles to his Jeep.

Barrett killed the engine and stepped out, unable to meet her gaze. He clutched his keys in his hand, torn between hearing her out and salvaging what was left of his dignity and leaving.

"You can't just say all of that and walk away from me!" Her voice wavered with emotion. "You were just going to leave without hearing what I had to say? You drop a bomb and walk away... like I mean *nothing*?"

"What do you want me to *say*, Chastity?" His voice boomed.

Several tenants peered out their curtains and blinds to see the show.

"I love you, too, Barrett. I have loved you since that night at the lake, maybe even before that. I didn't set out to play with your emotions. This has been hard on you. I *know* that. I was scared and confused. I shouldn't have pushed you away that day at your apartment. I should never have cost us a single day together because you're all I think about. But you gotta understand that I wanted you to have the *best* version of me. Not some fucked-up person who didn't know what she wanted or what she was doing. I know I've still got work on myself to do, but I want to do it with *you*. And… maybe it's too late for that."

She stepped away and turned. "If you still want to leave, I understand. But, Barrett… you have to know… I *need* you to know… that I am fucking crazy about you. I want to be with you. I want… *you*."

Barrett lunged forward, pulled her to him by the waist, and pressed a fevered kiss to her lips, parting them, clinging to her as if she was his only source of oxygen. She kissed him back in the dying light of the sun, their bodies casting twin shadows of hope on the asphalt.

Beside them, a car rolled up, headlights blasting. They simply ignored it, unwilling to let their long-awaited moment end for anyone else. When the car honked, they both blindly held up their middle fingers in its direction, tongues still making up for several months of lost time.

Minutes later, they crashed through the front door of her apartment. Barrett lowered her to the floor, kicking the front door shut behind them.

He climbed on top of her, mouth exploring the depths of hers. They stripped each other in a flurry, tossing shirts and belts and jeans everywhere as Molly sprawled all three of her long legs across the futon, watching them like a patient cuckold.

Barrett pushed Chastity's skirt up around her waist and tugged her lacy panties to the side. Grasping his rock-hard erection, Chastity moaned in anticipation, her face a beautiful shade of pink, lips red from friction.

Unable to stand it for another second, he buried himself inside of her, both groaning in satisfaction as the months of frustrating distance between them vanished.

Barrett watched her face, basking in the long-awaited feel of her warmth wrapped around him again, a sensation powerful enough to make him struggle not to cum right then and there.

Tears streaked down the sides of Chastity's temples. A brief smile graced her face, only to be replaced by a look of all-consuming pleasure as he slid in deeper.

Breathlessly, they stared into each other's eyes, and Barrett paused, never having felt closer to anyone in his life.

"I love you, Aphrodite."

Tears uninhibitedly streamed from the corners of her eyes, and she kissed him softly on the lips. "I love you, too."

"We can do this. We can do this right this time. We can make this work. I'll tell him I can't go to Denver."

"No," she said, voice full of certainty. She circled her pelvis beneath him, making his eyes roll back with pleasure. She pulled his head down and spoke lowly in his ear.

"*I'll come with you.*"

Barrett pulled back to look at her face. "What?"

"If you want."

"Of *course,* that's what I want." His smile was infectious.

"My lease is up in a few weeks. Barrett, we've spent enough time apart." She bit his bottom lip and circled her hips again. "I'm never fucking letting you go again."

He smiled and kissed her, his heart full. Now that they were together again, Barrett swore to himself that no matter where the path of life took them, it would take an actual act of God to pull them apart ever again.

Epilogue

Pulling a healthy blue orchid with fresh blooms from the moving box, Chastity set it gently on the bedroom windowsill of their new apartment. Cool fall rain dribbled down their window's cornice, obscuring the bustling activity of Denver in a gloomy hue of gray. Despite the chill of the autumn air outside, Chastity glistened with sweat and the remnants of rainwater as she unboxed more items, swishing her hips to a country song blasting through her phone speakers.

Barrett was due to come home at any minute.

Home.

The word still warmed her every time she thought about it.

Even after a few months of dating, the thought of seeing him still made her giddy. Her legs ached from lifting, kneeling, and, best of all, adventurous sex. They had christened every room of their apartment, except for their walk-in closet -- but she still had plans to change that.

Singing along with the tune, she unpacked a framed picture of her and her parents at her high school graduation. She hesitated before propping it up on an end table beside a picture of Barrett and his late grandmother. She flattened the box and tossed it on top of the pile of cardboard to be recycled.

It was official.

They were living together.

Cohabitating. Living in sin, as her parents would say.

But nothing about being with him felt sinful. Their life together was unconventional, and everything she dreamed loving someone could be.

Their modest, new place was already shaping up. The warm-colored bulbs in the inset fixtures bathed the place in a golden hue. Her sparse furniture blended well with his, and the leather and cream-colored walls gave off a cozy feeling. Glancing at the new appliances and freshly painted walls, she felt grateful Barrett earned such a comfortable wage at *Man Maid*. His job made their new life possible.

Molly sniffed the pile of boxes and looked at Chastity approvingly. She climbed on the leather couch and nestled her face into a couple of fluffy throw pillows Chastity had excitedly picked out with what little she had left from her last check and her half of the first, last, and security. She felt like an adult, finally living her life with someone who adored her just as she was.

It finally felt like she was in the right place at the right time. Barrett made her feel like she belonged.

Her job hunt had taken less time than she'd anticipated, thanks to a glowing recommendation from Marcy's dad at the bridal shop. Her new part-time gig at a similar boutique would provide just enough hours to help pay her half of the bills and grant her enough time to do her last semester of college over, finally earning her degree as a doctor in Veterinary Science. Her first day of work would start in two days, and her classes would begin the week after. Until then, all that lay between her and seeing what Denver had to offer was the rain.

Suddenly, the alarm on her phone went off. She stood still as stone, having momentarily forgotten about the test on the bathroom counter. She walked slowly as if she could sneak up on it and face reality at her own pace.

A wash of dread and excitement flowed through her in equal measure. She forced her feet to move across the plush carpet through their bedroom and into the *en suite* bathroom.

Her legs weakened at the sight. She grabbed onto the towel bar for support, wanting to crumble the moment she saw the results.

Two pink lines.

She buried her head in her hands, unsure whether to ugly-cry, puke, or scream with joy. Smoky wove her way through Chastity's legs, offering her warm, feline comfort in a moment of need. She lifted Smoky and held her against her chest, heart rate slowing at the sound of the animal's purr.

Just then, she heard the jingle of keys in the lock and the front door opening, soon followed by heavy footfalls.

"Wow!" He whistled. "Baby, the place looks amazing!"

She couldn't move, couldn't speak. Her body had shut down. Her legs were pillars of cement, eyes unable to focus on anything but the positive pregnancy test on the counter. She quickly tried to figure out what to do, what to say, but the thoughts jumbled in her head.

"Chastity?" he called, searching the apartment. She could hear the sly smile in his voice without even seeing it. "Where are you? I want to show my undying appreciation. In the *closet,* perhaps?"

If the situation had been any different, she would have laughed, but it suddenly seemed like the furthest thing from her mind.

She couldn't keep this from him. Maybe he had already sensed it.

Something in the air. A feeling.

He *had* to somehow know that their lives had just changed.

"Found you."

Her ears rang, barely registering the faint words from his lips.

After a few moments of clothes rustling nearby, Barrett tossed his briefs at her feet.

"*You. Closet. Now,*" he ordered playfully, like a sexy caveman.

When she didn't move, his tone suddenly changed.

"Baby? Something wrong? You alright?"

Without a word, Chastity broke out into a sob, clutching Smoky tighter against her chest. "I am so sorry."

"Whoa, what's wrong?" His voice was comforting as he wrapped her in a tight, naked embrace. "What are you sorry for? Did you break something? It's just stuff, we'll replace it."

Her teary eyes glanced down, and she nodded at the plastic stick balanced on the corner of the counter. Barrett followed her eyeline. His body suddenly grew rigid.

After a silence that must have lasted a full minute, another sob rocketed through Chastity's body.

Barrett broke out in a small chuckle. In a few moments, it grew louder. Before long, Chastity pulled away, glancing at him like a madman as his body shook with laughter.

He recomposed himself and looked her in the eyes, face pulled into a wide smile, eyes prickling with tears of his own. "I'm… gonna… be a Dad?" He hooted, his voice now an excited shout, "Oh my God! Chastity… we're gonna have a baby!?"

Chastity was stunned by his reaction.

"I… guess *so*."

Barrett shot away from her like a spring, sprinting excitedly around the apartment. "We're having a baby! Holy shit! What the… *how*? *When*? We've gotta… oh my *God*!"

Chastity followed the sound of his shouts.

"Ahhhh!" he screamed, followed by another deep laugh. The smile on his face was infectious.

Molly's eyes lazily watched Barrett's naked body dart across the apartment like a dog with the zoomies.

Reaching out to still him, Chastity felt a laugh bubble up in her own chest despite her simultaneous wash of terror.

His eyes widened, smile wiped away in an instant as her tears registered. "Oh, no, no, no. Please, Chastity… tell me you want to *keep* it."

After a moment, she nodded.

"*Yes!*" Barrett screamed, fist pumping toward the sky. He snatched up Smoky and held her in the air, hollering, "I'm gonna be a Daddy!"

Chastity looked down at his butt, at the tattoo of the bumble bee in a ghost costume on his firm cheek, and laughed through the tears. With parents like them, their child would certainly be *wild.*

Barrett placed the cat on the bed and scooped Chastity in his arms. "It's gonna be a boy. I can feel it!"

"*Barrett!*"

"I'll love it *whatever* it is!" The smile on his face was the biggest and brightest she'd ever seen in her life. "We're enrolling it in karate, especially if it's a girl. She's gonna be a dude-magnet."

"Let's not enroll our child in anything just yet. One thing at a time."

He blurted a joyful exclamation of sounds again and then clutched her arms in his hands. "This baby is going to be a part of you *and* me."

Her expression turned gravely serious. "That's what I'm worried about."

"Ouch. Okay, no offense taken, I guess," he said in a mocking tone, head bobbling with attitude.

She elbowed him gently in the ribs. "Not the part about *you*. I meant... what if she turns out like *me*?"

"What do you mean?" He paused. "Sassy and drop-dead gorgeous?"

"What if she's... *bipolar*?" Her voice wavered with concern, hands drifting down to her still-flat stomach.

"You mean *he's*," he joked. Then, his expression softened. He tucked a strand of hair behind her ear that had loosened from her multi-colored ponytail. "Then... nothing. I will love *her-him-it*, just like I love *you*. And who better to help our child through it than a mom who has dealt with the same thing head-on?"

He tipped her chin up and laid a gentle kiss on her lips. "You're brave. You're a badass. And you don't take shit from anyone. I'd be proud to watch our child grow up just like you."

"Thank you." She sniffled.

"Baby, I'm fucking *crazy* about you." He wrapped his arms around her, feeling the entirety of his world -- his past, present, and future -- all encompassed in them.

"*I love you*," she whispered into his neck, feeling anxiety give way to slight relief and even a little excitement. "If this anything like us, we're gonna have our hands full." She joked.

Molly sauntered over to Smoky's side. The contented animals stood, watching their enamored owners start a whole new adventure.

For the first time since she could remember, Chastity was surrounded by love and acceptance. The world spun in a way that finally made sense to her, some greater plan at play finally taking shape before her amber eyes.

Barrett knelt down to kiss her stomach, and Chastity giggled. Lifting her shirt, he spoke to her stomach. "Hello in there. I'm Barrett, but you can call me Daddy. I know we don't know each other, but I want you to know that I already love you, and I can't *wait* to meet you."

Author's Note

Chastity's journey was a lovely blend of many people, including myself, all wrapped in one beautiful, unmedicated package. Barrett was a fictionalized amalgamation of a few friends.

To Erica, my rock and my soulmate, thank you for being the hand that steers me in the right direction. As difficult as it must be to make our work shine sometimes, thank you for every single second you continue to spend on me. I know you only want the best for me. You always have and always will. Your work is beautiful and inspiring, and I learn from you every day.

To Carrie and Abi, thank you for your patience, your insight, and for helping me with my own bipolar diagnosis. You are both amazing. I couldn't have written this without you.

To my readers with mood disorders, if you suspect you may be dealing with something similar, do not be ashamed. Seeking help and maintaining a healthy lifestyle and balanced medication can change your life. Not everyone needs medication, but I am happy to report that they do not make you into some kind of zombie like I was told they would as a child. I am living proof that it will not curb your creative edge. I wrote this entire book while on medication for my bipolar. I've never had as much inspiration and hope as I do now. Being able to focus and step off of the emotional roller coaster has changed my life.

I also want to remind those of you with mood disorders that the world is still a *much* better place *because* you are in it. The world needs your sunshine.

To my fellow Christians, this story was not intended as an attack on our faith. As a woman who is deeply faithful, so much of writing this was a reality check. We all have struggles. The harder we push, the more people rebel sometimes. Faith, to me, is about loving everyone as they are and treating them with the love and respect they deserve. I pray this story is taken as a humbling reminder to love God's children without judgment.

God bless you all, and thank you for reading.

About the Author

Aurora Alba is an award-winning author of contemporary and paranormal romance. She also writes fantasy, horror, and mystery under the pen names Heather Wohl and H.M. Wohl.

She hails from a small town in Wyoming and writes with the full support of her husband and fur-babies. She strives to be a captivating storyteller. Love, in all forms, is her passion.

Reviews

If you could take the time to leave an honest review after you've read this book, we at Rusty Ogre Publishing would *greatly* appreciate it. We respect your time and promise it doesn't *have* to be long and eloquent. Even a few words will do!

As a small publishing house, every review helps others determine if this book is right for them and greatly increases our chances of being discovered by someone else who might enjoy it.

A Note From The Ogres

Even though this book was proofread thoroughly by editors, beta readers, and ARC readers... mistakes happen. We want our readers to have the best experience possible. If you spot any spelling, grammatical, or formatting errors, please feel free to reach out and let us know at:

Rustyogrepublishing@gmail.com

More From Rusty Ogre

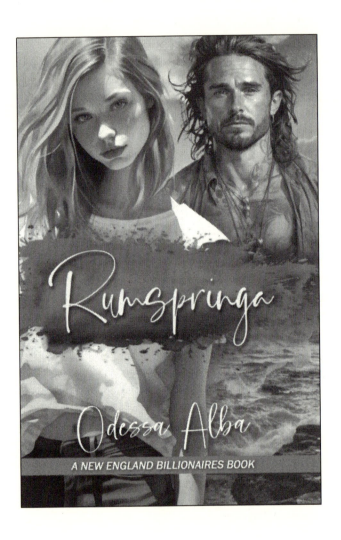

Rumspringa

Odessa Alba

A NEW ENGLAND BILLIONAIRES BOOK

The Ugly Sweater PARTY

A FORCED PROXIMITY ROMANCE NOVELLA

AURORA ALBA &
ODESSA ALBA

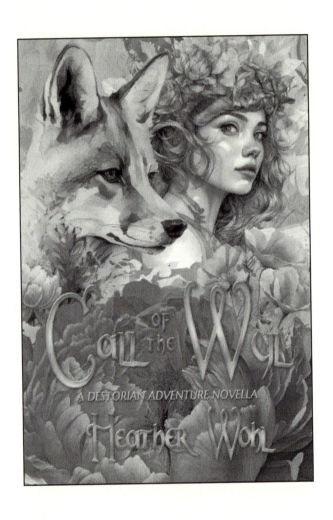

Call of the Wyld

A DESTORIAN ADVENTURE NOVELLA

Heather Won

Maid
for You
BOOK THREE OF THE MAN MAID SERIES
FROM AWARD-WINNING AUTHOR
AURORA ALBA

Tangled Heirs

Odessa Alba

A NEW ENGLAND BILLIONAIRES BOOK

Made in the USA
Middletown, DE
25 February 2025

71870488R00224